RUTH

EXPERIENCING A LIFE RESTORED

A Bible study based
on the teaching of

———

NANCY DeMOSS
WOLGEMUTH

© 2021 *Revive Our Hearts*
First printing, 2021

Published by *Revive Our Hearts*
P.O. Box 2000, Niles, MI 49120

ISBN: 978-1-934718-79-7

Printed in the United States of America.

Adapted from the teaching of Nancy DeMoss Wolgemuth by Mindy Kroesche, edited by Laura Elliott, Erin Davis, Micayla Brickner, and Katie Laitkep.

As you work through this study, use this space to doodle, color, and meditate on God's Word and consider how the story of Ruth gives you true hope.

FOR WHATEVER WAS WRITTEN IN *former days* WAS WRITTEN FOR OUR INSTRUCTION *that through* endurance *and through the* ENCOURAGEMENT OF THE SCRIPTURES *we might have* HOPE.

Romans 15:4

Ruth's Story

AS FOUND IN RUTH 1

[1] In the days when the judges ruled there was a famine in the land, and a man of Bethlehem in Judah went to sojourn in the country of Moab, he and his wife and his two sons. [2] The name of the man was Elimelech and the name of his wife Naomi, and the names of his two sons were Mahlon and Chilion. They were Ephrathites from Bethlehem in Judah. They went into the country of Moab and remained there. [3] But Elimelech, the husband of Naomi, died, and she was left with her two sons. [4] These took Moabite wives; the name of the one was Orpah and the name of the other Ruth. They lived there about ten years, [5] and both Mahlon and Chilion died, so that the woman was left without her two sons and her husband.

RUTH'S LOYALTY TO NAOMI

[6] Then she arose with her daughters-in-law to return from the country of Moab, for she had heard in the fields of Moab that the LORD had visited his people and given them food. [7] So she set out from the place where she was with her two daughters-in-law, and they went on the way to return to the land of Judah. [8] But Naomi said to her two daughters-in-law, "Go, return each of you

to her mother's house. May the LORD deal kindly with you, as you have dealt with the dead and with me. ⁹ The LORD grant that you may find rest, each of you in the house of her husband!" Then she kissed them, and they lifted up their voices and wept. ¹⁰And they said to her, "No, we will return with you to your people." ¹¹ But Naomi said, "Turn back, my daughters; why will you go with me? Have I yet sons in my womb that they may become your husbands? ¹² Turn back, my daughters; go your way, for I am too old to have a husband. If I should say I have hope, even if I should have a husband this night and should bear sons, ¹³ would you therefore wait till they were grown? Would you therefore refrain from marrying? No, my daughters, for it is exceedingly bitter to me for your sake that the hand of the LORD has gone out against me." ¹⁴ Then they lifted up their voices and wept again. And Orpah kissed her mother-in-law, but Ruth clung to her.

¹⁵ And she said, "See, your sister-in-law has gone back to her people and to her gods; return after your sister-in-law." ¹⁶ But Ruth said, "Do not urge me to leave you or to return from following you. For where you go I will go, and where you lodge I will lodge. Your people shall be my people, and your God my God. ¹⁷ Where you die I will die, and there will I be buried. May the LORD do so to me and more also if anything but death parts me from you." ¹⁸ And when Naomi saw that she was determined to go with her, she said no more.

NAOMI AND RUTH RETURN

¹⁹ So the two of them went on until they came to Bethlehem. And when they came to Bethlehem, the whole town was stirred because of them. And the women said, "Is this Naomi?" ²⁰ She said to them, "Do not call me Naomi; call me Mara, for the Almighty has dealt very bitterly with me. ²¹ I went away full, and the LORD has brought me back empty. Why call me Naomi, when the LORD has testified against me and the Almighty has brought calamity upon me?"

²² So Naomi returned, and Ruth the Moabite her daughter-in-law with her, who returned from the country of Moab. And they came to Bethlehem at the beginning of barley harvest.

A suffering nation, reeling from famine, judgment, and war, Israel was a dark and unfriendly home for most, *particularly for a woman*. Even more so for a widowed woman. Ruth's story begins in desolation. But as in every story whose Author is God, that desolation is not without a glimmer of hope.

As you watch that glimmer of hope bloom into a dazzling display of grace, you'll understand why the book of Ruth is called, by some, the greatest love story of all time. But this love story is much less about *romance* and more about *restoration*. It's a story of how God can turn tragedy into joy, no matter how desperate our circumstances may seem.

While the book of Ruth contains the story of wanderers coming home, mourning turned into dancing, and desperation shifting to celebration, most of all it illustrates the redeeming and restoring love of Jesus, who takes the broken pieces of our lives and turns them into a thing of beauty.

WHAT YOU CAN EXPECT TO LEARN

Expect these five themes to deeply embed themselves in your heart through this study:

- **Hope.** We'll see how God turns hopeless situations to joy, how He brings beauty out of ashes. God can restore even the most desperate situations of life.
- **Love.** Ruth is one of the most beautiful love stories of all time. We'll see that true love is more than just romance—it's unconditional, sacrificial, and lasting.

- **Relationships.** Through Ruth, we will see how relationships can be healed and made whole through God's restorative power.
- **Rest.** Through Naomi's search for rest for herself and her daughters-in-law, we'll see that rest isn't a matter of a change in our external circumstances but something God gives within our hearts.
- **Restoration.** As we walk through this book with Ruth, Naomi, and Boaz, we'll see how Christ can redeem and restore our lives in a way that overrules the losses and failures caused by our sins.

TIPS FOR USING THIS STUDY

As you use this study, ask yourself:

- What does this passage teach me about the heart, ways, and character of God?
- How does this passage point to Jesus and the gospel?
- Is there an example for me to follow or avoid? If so, how should I seek to change?

Each week of study is divided into five suggested daily lessons, but feel free to work at your own pace. Do what works for you!

You may also find it beneficial to listen to the audio series "Ruth and the Transforming Power of Redeeming Love" at ReviveOurHearts.com/Ruth.

The Holy Spirit helps us understand God's Word. He is a gift and a "Helper" who is able to "teach you all things and bring to your remembrance all that I [Jesus] have said to you" (John 14:26).

Secondary tools that can help you better understand the Word of God (but aren't necessary) include:

- An English dictionary to look up the basic meaning of words
- Various translations of the Bible (a good online tool is BibleGateway.com)
- A concordance
- A Bible dictionary
- Commentaries
- A study Bible
- Colored pens or pencils to write in your Bible

We've included group discussion questions at the end of this book. Join the discussion about Ruth with the *Women of the Bible* podcast created to accompany this study. Find it at ReviveOurHearts.com/WomenoftheBible.

OUR HOPE FOR YOU

Over the next six weeks, the *Revive Our Hearts* team hopes you:

- Find practical wisdom to apply to your daily life.
- Read your Bible with greater passion.
- Experience the wonder of your own restoration.
- Rediscover that every story is really God's story, *even yours.*
- Know God better as a result of this study.

Spend time meditating on and memorizing the following verse this week:

To grant to those who mourn in Zion— to give them a *beautiful* HEADDRESS instead of ashes, the oil of *gladness* instead of MOURNING.

ISAIAH 61:3

Week 1

BEAUTY FROM ASHES

Big Idea: WE ARE ALL DESPERATE AND NEED RESTORATION.

INTRODUCTION

What comes to mind when you think of ashes? Perhaps something gray and gritty, smoky and dirty, the residue of an item that's been destroyed. Maybe it's the rubble you sweep from a fireplace and throw out in the trash. Whatever comes to mind, ashes probably aren't something you associate with beauty.

As we open the book of Ruth, Naomi's life seems to be nothing but ashes—at least looking at it from her perspective. Far from her homeland in a culture that didn't worship the one true God, her husband, dead, along with her two sons, Naomi's life was full of tragedy; her situation looked hopeless. Yes, she had her two daughters-in-law, but how could three women alone in ancient Israel provide for each other?

"But God" (two of the most beautiful words in the Bible!) had a different plan. He took the ashes of Naomi's life and made something beautiful. He used Naomi's story to showcase His power to restore, even when restoration seemed impossible.

Day 1: *A Desperate Situation*

Read Ruth 1:1–18.

The book of Ruth is one of two books in the Bible named after a woman (the other is Esther). The writer of Ruth focuses on two women: Ruth and her mother-in-law, Naomi. Both women were widowed. Beyond the emotional toll such losses must have taken, they likely also found themselves financially destitute. As a result, they left the country of Moab to return to Naomi's homeland of Israel.

Over the next six weeks, as we walk through Ruth together, we'll take time to dive deeply into this book. For now let's get an overview.

Overview of the Book of Ruth

Author:
The Bible does not say who wrote Ruth. The Talmud (Jewish tradition) points to Samuel as the author. However, other scholars speculate that Nathan, Solomon, or someone else wrote this book.[1]

When:
The events in the book of Ruth took place during the last part of the period of judges, sometime between 1160 BC and 1100 BC. [2]

Where:
The first part of Ruth occurred in the country of Moab, located east of the Dead Sea. The rest of the story of Ruth took place in Bethlehem in Judah.

Reread Ruth 1:1–5.

List the words that come to mind to describe Naomi's situation.

-
-
-
-

Have you ever been in a desperate situation and been tempted to think, *How could anything good ever come out of this?*

_____

_____

_____

_____

_____

Think about instances in the Bible where God's people were desperate. List some of those situations. (We've listed a couple to get you started.)

- Israel turned to God in desperation (2 Chron. 15:3–4).
- King David cried out to God when his son was sick (2 Sam. 12:15–17).
-
-

Ruth's story is a beautiful reminder that even our darkest circumstances can be redeemed. Because of God's faithfulness, there will be joy at the end of every heartache. There will be beauty out of the ashes.

What parts of your story feel like "ashes" right now?

_____

_____

_____

Take time to meditate on Isaiah 61:1–3 below, then write a short prayer asking God to give you hope that He can turn your ashes into something beautiful.

> The Spirit of the Lord God is upon me,
>   because the Lord has anointed me
> to bring good news to the poor;
>   he has sent me to bind up the brokenhearted,
> to proclaim liberty to the captives,
>   and the opening of the prison to those who are bound;
>
> to proclaim the year of the Lord's favor,
>   and the day of vengeance of our God;
>   to comfort all who mourn;
> to grant to those who mourn in Zion—
>   to give them a beautiful headdress instead of ashes,
> the oil of gladness instead of mourning.

Day 2: *Meet the Cast*

Read Ruth 2:1–21.

While this book is named after Ruth, she's not the only character in the story. Ruth, Naomi, and Boaz all play prominent parts, with a few others filling out important supporting roles. Ultimately, however, the book of Ruth is a story about God.

Revisit Ruth 1:1–2 and sketch a family tree of the people mentioned.

The names on this family tree may give us insight into the story. Throughout the Bible, a person's name is often symbolic, revealing something about his or her character, situation, or aspirations (or perhaps the aspirations of his or her parents!). Here is a list of names from the book of Ruth and their potential meanings.

Name	Potential Meaning
Elimelech	"My God is King"[3]
Mahlon	"Sickly"[4]
Chilion	"Wasting away"[5]
Orpah	"Neck" or "fawn"[6]

On to our three main characters: Naomi, Ruth, and Boaz. Give a brief description of each of these individuals using words, drawings, word art, or a combination. Be creative!

Naomi

Ruth

Boaz

In Hebrew, Naomi's name means "pleasantness,"[7] Ruth means "friend,"[8] and Boaz means "fleetness" or "swiftness."[9] Are there any ways that the meaning of their names is evident in our reading for today?

_____

_____

_____

Review Ruth 1:19–21 and record the new name Naomi gave herself. What did this new name mean?

_____

_____

_____

We will learn to love this cast of characters over the next six weeks, but their stories point us to the Director of *every story,* God. We'll see more clearly all the little incidents and details throughout the book of Ruth in which, from a human standpoint, restoration seemed impossible . . . "but God."

Make a list of the "cast" in your own life. Next to each name write out a brief prayer about an area where you're asking the Lord to bring restoration.

Cast Member   Prayer for Restoration

Day 3: *In the Days When the Judges Ruled*

Reread Ruth 1:1.

The first phrase of the first verse of Ruth tells us something important about the setting of this story—"in the days when the judges ruled."

The judges were those who ruled over Israel after the death of Joshua. Joshua was a spiritual and military leader. He followed in the footsteps of his mentor, Moses, who led God's people out of slavery in Egypt. During Joshua's lifetime, the people had seen the works of God—they had been delivered from slavery, walked through the parted Red Sea, and been led through the wilderness. They saw the power of God that took them into Canaan, conquered foreign nations, and gave them the Promised Land.

After Joshua and his peers died, however, a new generation was in place.

Read Judges 2:6–13 and compare the people during Joshua's time and during the days of the next generation.

Joshua's generation (v. 7):   The next generation (vv.10–13):

Verse 13 says that the Israelites "abandoned the LORD and served the Baals and the Ashtaroth."

This is a reference to the Canaanite gods. Canaan was an agricultural economy, and in order for the people to be prosperous, two things had to be fertile: the land, so they could have crops, and their wives, so they could have laborers to work the crops.

The Canaanites' chief god was called Baal. That word means "lord or owner,"[10] and the Canaanites believed that Baal owned the land and controlled fertility. Ashtoreth was believed to be Baal's female partner.

The Canaanites believed that the fertility of the land and of their women was the result of sexual activity between the gods. In order to get the gods in heaven to do what the Canaanites wanted on earth, the people would go up to hills, called high places, and perform the sexual acts they wanted the gods to perform in heaven. They believed this would make the land and the women fertile.

Over time, the Israelites became assimilated into this culture and began to practice these same sins.

What evidence do you see of spiritual darkness in our culture? Make a list.

_____

_____

_____

According to verses 14–15, what was God's response to Israel's sin?

_____

_____

_____

The book of Judges ends with this description of the culture in Israel:

> In those days there was no king in Israel. Everyone did what was right in his own eyes. (JUDG. 21:25)

Ruth lived in dark days; cultural and spiritual darkness surrounded her. Choosing righteousness couldn't have been easy for her. It's not easy for us. However, the story of Ruth can give us confidence that it's possible to walk with God in our workplaces, with our families, in our churches and communities even when cultural and spiritual darkness are pervasive.

In Philippians 2:15, the apostle Paul shares the reason why we're to live for God in a world that doesn't love Him or acknowledge Him. Write out the verse below, then underline that purpose.

_____

_____

_____

Read Matthew 5:14–16. Draw a picture illustrating how God calls us to live in our dark world.

Day 4: *You Can Run, But You Can't Hide*

Reread Ruth 1:1–2.

Do you ever find yourself wanting to run from pressure? The real question might be "which day *don't* I feel like this?" The temptation in the midst of pressure, pain, or problems—whether big or small—is to want to escape from the realities of life. As we see in the story of Ruth, we're not the only ones to feel this way.

What difficulty was happening in Israel at the start of the book of Ruth (v. 1)?

_____

_____

What is a famine?

_____

_____

Although there are many reasons famines can happen, Scripture tells us that sometimes God allows famine for a specific purpose. In Deuteronomy 30:15–18, God made an agreement with the Israelites. He promised that if they obeyed Him, they would be blessed. They would have families and the land would produce crops. If they disobeyed His laws, there would be natural consequences of their disobedience, like famine and hunger, military oppression, etc.

Read the passages below that describe famines experienced by the nation of Israel. Underline the description of the famine. Double underline *why* God allowed each famine to occur.

"And if in spite of this you will not listen to me, then I will discipline you again sevenfold for your sins, and I will break the pride of your power, and I will make your heavens like iron and your earth like bronze. And your strength shall be spent in vain, for your land shall not yield its increase, and the trees of the land shall not yield their fruit."
(LEV. 26:18-20)

"But if you will not obey the voice of the LORD your God or be careful to do all his commandments and his statutes that I command you today, then all these curses shall come upon you and overtake you. Cursed shall you be in the city, and cursed shall you be in the field. Cursed shall be your basket and your kneading bowl. Cursed shall be the fruit of your womb and the fruit of your ground, the increase of your herds and the young of your flock. . . . And the heavens over your head shall be bronze, and the earth under you shall be iron. The LORD will make the rain of your land powder. From heaven dust shall come down on you until you are destroyed." (DEUT. 28:15-18, 23-24)

In each of these famines, God used natural disasters to restore His people to a place of obedience. We don't know if the famine Elimelech's family experienced in Bethlehem was God's judgment or not. We do know how Elimelech chose to respond.

Fleeing the Famine

In response to the famine, Elimelech chose to leave his homeland of Bethlehem in Judah and go to the neighboring country of Moab. Moab was approximately sixty miles from Bethlehem on the other side of the Dead Sea.

Match the following passages with what they tell us about Moab and the people who lived there.

Genesis 19:36–37

When the Israelites sinned, God let Moab defeat them and rule over them.

Numbers 25:1–4

The Moabites worshiped Chemosh, a false God.

Judges 3:12–14

They were descended from Lot's incestuous relationship with one of his daughters.

2 Kings 23:13

God was angry at Israel for following the practice of the Moabites including sacrificing to other gods.

The Moabites were the enemies of the Israelites. They worshiped false and evil gods (Num. 25:2). Despite generations of tension between Moab and Israel, Elimelech chose to leave his homeland and escape to neighboring Moab.

Revisit Ruth 1:1. What word is used to describe their travel to Moab? _____

What does this reveal about Elimelech's intentions for his family's time in Moab?

_____

_____

_____

Approximately how long did they stay? (vv. 2–5)

_____

_____

_____

We don't know whether Elimelech was trying to escape God's judgment by fleeing to Moab. We don't know whether it would have been better for him to stay and repent. We *do* know that even in enemy territory, even during a famine, Elimelech could not escape God's plan for his family.

Where Are You Running?

What circumstances do you wish you could just run away from right now?

_____

_____

_____

What do you tend to run toward in the midst of hardship to try and find relief? Food, shopping, social media, work, friends, something else?

_____

_____

_____

How has God used difficult circumstances to cause you to turn to Him?

_____

_____

_____

Scripture tells us that there were times when King David, the man after God's own heart (1 Sam. 13:14), wanted to run away, too.

Psalm 55 describes a time when David was dealing with his enemies and had been betrayed by someone he thought was a close friend. In your own words describe David's words recorded in Psalm 55:6–8.

_____

_____

_____

_____

_____

We don't get an indication from this psalm that David was able to escape his troubles, but verse 16 represents a shift in David's tone. Read verses 16–19 and 22 below. Circle the phrases that indicate what David relied on in this time of hardship.

> But I call to God,
>   and the LORD will save me.
> Evening and morning and at noon
>   I utter my complaint and moan,
>   and he hears my voice.
> He redeems my soul in safety
>   from the battle that I wage,
>   for many are arrayed against me.
> God will give ear and humble them,
>   he who is enthroned from of old. *Selah*
> because they do not change
>   and do not fear God. . . .
> Cast your burden on the LORD,
>   and he will sustain you;
> he will never permit
>   the righteous to be moved. (VV. 16-19, 22)

What was He trusting God to do?

_____

_____

To close today's study, meditate on Psalm 139:7–12. This passage is a reminder that we can never outrun God. Even in the spiritually dark nation of Moab, Elimelech could not outrun God's plan for His family. How does it comfort you to know you cannot outrun God's plans for your life?

_____

_____

_____

Day 5: *Alone, but Not Abandoned*

Reread Ruth 1:3–5.

Today's passage describes the events in Naomi's life very plainly—as a matter-of-fact. Beneath the words, however, we can feel the currents of pain. Naomi had lost her whole family. She was left destitute. She was in an extremely difficult and painful situation.

Based on what you've learned about her life, what emotions do you think Naomi was likely wrestling with?

-
-
-
-

Did "abandoned" make your list? Do you think that Naomi may have felt like God had abandoned her? Why or why not?

_____

_____

_____

Have you ever felt like God abandoned you? Write honestly about that experience.

_____

_____

_____

_____

_____

Throughout Scripture, we find multiple examples of people who were going through a difficult time. They most likely felt like God was far away. Yet He was working through their situation for a purpose.

Match each person from Scripture with the trial they went through.

Bible Character	Trial Faced
Joseph (Gen. 37:12–36; 39:11–20; 50:15–21)	Could not have children.
	Thrown in prison for teaching others about Jesus.
Job (Job 1:13–19; 2:7; 42:1–6)	
Hannah (1 Sam. 1)	Lost his property, children, and health.
Paul (Acts 28:17–30; Phil. 1:13)	Betrayed by his brothers and unjustly thrown into prison.

Choose one of the characters from this list. Imagine yourself in his or her shoes. What emotions would you be feeling?

_____

_____

_____

Psalm 22 is another psalm of David. Read verses 1–2 and rewrite them in your own words.

_____

_____

_____

Based on what you read, do you think David felt abandoned by God? Why or why not?

_____

_____

_____

Jesus quoted this psalm as He hung on the cross. Read Matthew 27:45–50. In your Bible, underline the words that come from Psalm 22 or write them in the space below.

_____

_____

_____

Jesus was in an extremely difficult situation—physically, emotionally, and spiritually. He was hanging on a cross for a crime He hadn't committed, abandoned by His friends and followers. Do you think He felt abandoned by God the Father? Why or why not?

_____

_____

_____

Look up the following verses:

DEUTERONOMY 31:6, 8

HEBREWS 13:5-6

What do these passages promise for God's children?

_____

_____

_____

Use the paraphrase you wrote for Psalm 22:1–2 as a starting point to talk to God about the times you've felt abandoned by Him. Be completely honest about your feelings and your fears. Then ask Him to give you assurance of His presence as you reflect on His character and the knowledge that He has promised to never leave you or forsake you.

_____

_____

_____

_____

_____

_____

_____

Spend time meditating on and memorizing the following verse this week:

Where you go I will go, and where you lodge I will lodge. Your people shall be my people, and your God my God. Where you die I will die, and there will I be buried. May the Lord do so to me and more also if anything but death parts me from you.

RUTH 1:16-17

Week 2

Big Idea: IT'S NEVER TOO LATE TO CHOOSE TO LIVE FOR GOD.

INTRODUCTION

Imagine you're driving home from a long trip. You decide to try a different route and enjoy some new scenery. The GPS says it should take about six hours. After four and a half hours of driving, you realize you're on the wrong road, one that's taken you almost the opposite direction of where you wanted to be. Would you just shrug your shoulders and keep on going? Of course not! You'd turn that car around and start in the right direction. How long the trip takes is no longer important. You need to get back where you belong.

When we've strayed from God's plan for us, it might be easy to think we're too far gone to turn around. Yet it doesn't matter how much we mess up; God is waiting for us to come to our senses, repent of our sin, and get back on the right path of following Him. This week, we'll see Naomi take her first step on that long journey. She didn't know what awaited her at the end of the road; she just knew that Moab wasn't where she was supposed to be.

Whether you're coming back to the Lord from a far-off place or continuing along the path of following Him, may our study this week encourage you to stay the course. The commitment to follow Jesus isn't always easy, but the joy and rest we find in Him is completely worth it.

Day 1: *Too Far Gone?*

Read 1 Timothy 1:12–17.

Last week we learned that God would sometimes send a famine as a means of discipline for the Israelites (Deut. 28) in order to cause his people to turn back to Him (Amos 4:6–11). What if the Israelites felt they were too far gone—that they couldn't turn back and follow God because their sins were too "big"?

Have you ever felt that way? That your sin was too big for God to forgive or you had wandered too far from Him to come back? Describe the situation below.

_____

_____

_____

The Bible is full of examples of people we might describe as "too far gone." But God in His mercy and grace provided a different outcome to their stories than what we may have predicted.

Let's look at two examples in Acts 7:58–8:3 and Mark 5:1–5 of people who were far away from following Jesus. Note: as you read these accounts, imagine this is your first time hearing them even if you're already familiar with the stories.

With only the information provided in the above verses, on a scale of 1–10 how likely do you think it was for these individuals to follow Jesus?

HIGHLY UNLIKELY   SOMEWHAT LIKELY   HIGHLY LIKELY

| 1 | 2 | 3 | 4 | 5 | 6 | 7 | 8 | 9 | 10 |

Now let's see how the rest of these stories played out. Read Acts 9:1–22 and Mark 5:6–20.

In each passage, what was the catalyst for change in the individual's life?

_____

_____

_____

What surprised you the most in each instance?

_____

_____

_____

In our human thinking, the lives of Saul and the demon-possessed man seem as if they're too far gone and could never change. However, God knew better. Both of these men were without hope in and of themselves—as we all are. Romans 3:23 tells us, "For all have sinned and fall short of the glory of God." But as the next verse says, that's why God sent His Son, Jesus, that we might be "justified [made right with God] by his grace as a gift, through the redemption that is in Christ Jesus" (v. 24).

Match the following passages with the description of what Jesus did for us when we were far away from Him.

Isaiah 53:6   Even though He never sinned, He became
                                     sin for our sake.

John 3:16–18   He paid the price for our guilt and sin.

2 Corinthians 5:21   He carried the load of our sins so that we
                                     can be free.

1 Peter 2:24   He gave us eternal life and freed us from
                                     condemnation.

31

Because God is holy, His justice requires punishment for every sin. You and I cannot pay that debt. There is only one remedy for our guilt, and that is the blood of Jesus Christ. When Jesus came and offered Himself as a sacrifice, He did it once for all so that the penalty for our sin was permanently paid.

You might know this truth in your head. Yet maybe you find it hard to believe in your heart—that God really offers you His love and forgiveness no matter what you've done.

The Bible says that when you "confess with your mouth that Jesus is Lord and believe in your heart that God raised him from the dead, you will be saved" (Rom. 10:9). And that "if anyone is in Christ, he is a new creation. The old has passed away; behold, the new has come" (2 Cor. 5:17). It's not based on anything that we have or haven't done; rather it's a gift from God (Eph. 2:8–9).

For more perspective, let's go back to one of our examples, the apostle Paul (formerly known as Saul, whom we read about in Acts).

How would you describe Paul before his encounter with Christ?

_____

_____

_____

Reread 1 Timothy 1:12–17.

How did Paul describe himself?

_____

_____

_____

According to verse 16, why does Paul say that God chose to show him mercy?

_____

_____

Paul was specific and honest about his past. He wasn't proud of it, but he viewed it as a showcase for God's grace—that others would see how God had transformed his life and have hope that they, too, could be forgiven, no matter how great their sins may be.

As you think about your own story, how can God use you to point others to His mercy and forgiveness?

_____

_____

_____

In verse 17, Paul ends his testimony of how God saved him by saying, "To the King of the ages, immortal, invisible, the only God, be honor and glory forever and ever. Amen."

Does this sound like someone who is still living under the guilt and shame of his past? Why or why not?

_____

_____

_____

Paul was a man who was free; the penalty for his sin had been paid. The blood of Jesus covered Paul's sin—and it covers yours, too. When you've been forgiven by God, when you've been washed by the blood of Jesus, you are totally free. There is no sin so great that God can't forgive.

In Colossians 2:13–14, Paul wrote:

> And you, who were dead in your trespasses and the uncircumcision of your flesh, God made alive together with him, having forgiven us all our trespasses, by canceling the record of debt that stood against us with its legal demands. This he set aside, nailing it to the cross.

On the picture of the cross below, write any sins you feel are "too big" for God to forgive. Just as these notes are nailed to this cross, if you are a child of God your sins have been nailed to *the* cross and are forgiven forever.

Day 2: *The Road to Repentance*

Read Ruth 1:6-7.

At the beginning of our passage today, Naomi was preparing to finally leave Moab and go back home to Bethlehem.

What did Naomi learn that motivated her to return?

_____

_____

_____

Naomi was living in a land where the inhabitants had a long history of following a false god rather than the one true God. Her choice to return home paints for us *a picture of repentance*—choosing to turn from sin and wrong choices and live for God instead. What do the following verses have to say about repentance?

2 CHRONICLES 7:14 _____

_____

ACTS 3:19 _____

_____

1 JOHN 1:9 _____

_____

The Greek word for "repent" in Acts 3:19 is *metanoia.* *Meta* means "to change" and *noia* means "the mind." Repentance is a change of thinking about ourselves, our sin, and God, which results in a change of heart and life.

Repentance is a change from the inside out; it's both internal and external. It affects every part of us. When we repent, we're changing direction, turning away from the attitudes and values we once had and turning toward God instead. With this definition in mind, draw a picture that represents true repentance in the space below.

While repentance is a change of mind, it should also be visible in our behavior. When we're truly repentant, our lives will show evidence of that change (Matt. 3:8).

What are signs of repentance in someone's life? Match the following verses with their description of repentance.

Joel 2:12–13   Accepting the consequences of our actions

Luke 19:1–10   Sorrow over our sin

Luke 23:40–41   A change in behavior

Acts 9   Desire to make restitution

In his second letter to the church in Corinth, the apostle Paul gave more clues to help us know if we've truly repented. As you read the passage, circle the words "sorrow" and "sorrowful" every time they appear.

> For though I caused you sorrow by my letter, I do not regret it; though I did regret it—*for* I see that that letter caused you sorrow, though only for a while—I now rejoice, not that you were made sorrowful, but that you were made sorrowful to *the point* of repentance; for you were made sorrowful according to *the will of* God, so that you might not suffer loss in anything through us. For the sorrow that is according to *the will of* God produces a repentance without regret, *leading* to salvation, but the sorrow of the world produces death. For behold what earnestness this very thing, this godly sorrow, has produced in you: what vindication *of yourselves*, what indignation, what fear, what longing, what zeal, what punishment of wrong! In everything you demonstrated yourselves to be innocent in the matter. (2 COR. 7:8-11 NASB)

What is the connection between repentance and sorrow?

_____

_____

How have you experienced this in your own life?

_____

_____

_____

Repentance is just the beginning of the process of restoration. In Naomi's life, it was a long road back home. There was no quick route to Judah. Again, we can apply this as an object lesson for our own lives. There is no quick fix for us when we've gone into our Moab, away from the will of God. There is a road back home from rebellion to restoration.

Repentance requires a willingness to walk that road.

Have you had a Moab, an area of sin, from which you've walked away from?

_____

_____

_____

What are the signs that show you've truly repented and turned toward the Lord?

_____

_____

_____

Tomorrow we'll explore more in-depth what it means to repent and return to following God. Take some time now to ask God to prepare your heart to hear His voice as we continue our study.

Day 3: *Return to Me*

Read Joel 2:12–14.

Yesterday we saw how Naomi's choice to return to Bethlehem was like getting on the road of repentance. Yet imagine if she had stopped halfway and said, "This road is too long. I'm too old. I don't think I want to make this trek." Her attachment to people in Moab could have made her go halfway and say, "I think I'm going back."

In our lives, Moab represents those people, places, or things that we may have turned to in an effort to get our needs met. We've tried to use them as a substitute for God in our lives. As you look back on your life, you may be able to point to a time of spiritual famine or hardship where you tried to fill the emptiness with something that was man-made rather than looking to God. *You settled for a substitute.*

Often, we stay off the road to repentance because it's uncomfortable. We seek the familiar instead. Make a list of the comforts you tend to run to in times of difficulty rather than going to God.

_____

_____

_____

What appeal do these things hold for you?

_____

_____

What should we do when we've been running to places other than God? How do we get back home? As you read the passages below, underline any words or phrases they have in common.

> And Samuel said to all the house of Israel, "If you are returning to the Lord with all your heart, then put away the foreign gods and the Ashtaroth from among you and direct your heart to the Lord and serve him only, and he will deliver you out of the hand of the Philistines." (1 SAM. 7:3)

> "I will give them a heart to know that I am the Lord, and they shall be my people and I will be their God, for they shall return to me with their whole heart." (JER. 24:7)

> Return, O Israel, to the Lord your God,
>   for you have stumbled because of your iniquity. (HOS. 14:1)

> Return to the Lord your God,
>   for he is gracious and merciful,
> slow to anger, and abounding in steadfast love;
>   and he relents over disaster. (JOEL 2:13)

> "Therefore say to them, Thus declares the Lord of hosts: Return to me, says the Lord of hosts, and I will return to you, says the Lord of hosts." (ZECH. 1:3)

What is God asking His people to do?

_____

_____

_____

Over and over throughout the Old Testament, we find the message of *return*. God says to His people, "Yes, you've wandered, but I want you to come back to Me."

When we repent, we're really saying, "Jesus, I'm coming home to You. I'm coming to a place of obedience and surrender, confessing that You are the One who satisfies me and meets my needs."

Sometimes, we become so comfortable in our sin that we lose our desire to leave it. Maybe our Moab is nothing more than dwelling on bitter feelings or sharing a little gossip. What was intended as a *visit* has become a *lifestyle*.

Does this describe a current situation in your life? If so, have you come to the place where you're willing to leave what's become comfortable to get on a different road?

To help you get started, pray through the following steps:

1. Respond. Your desire to return to God is an indication that He is at work in your heart. Thank God for lovingly calling you to return to intimacy with Him.

2. Confess. Be specific about your sin and accept responsibility for the choices you have made.

3. Ask. Ask God to give you a godly sorrow that leads to repentance (2 Cor. 7:10). It's an unpleasant step in an ultimately victorious journey.

4. Adjust. What adjustments do you need to make to put this sin out of your life?

The time to respond is when God speaks. Leave your Moab today. It won't be any easier tomorrow. In the following space, write a prayer to God involving the steps of repentance that He took you through today.

I respond . . . _____

_____

_____

I confess . . . _____

_____

_____

I ask . . . _____

_____

_____

Help me to adjust . . . _____

_____

_____

Day 4: *Seeking Rest*

Read Ruth 1:8–9.

When Naomi decided to return to Israel, she headed out with her daughters-in-law traveling with her. Somewhere along the journey, however, she tried to persuade them to turn back.

In the end of verse 9, what does Naomi say she wants for Orpah and Ruth?

_____

_____

_____

The word *rest* is found in the book of Ruth several times. Naomi was seeking rest, not only for her soul but for her bereaved daughters-in-law. Perhaps she thought the only place they would find that rest was under the shelter of another husband.

The Hebrew word that Naomi uses for rest here is *měnuwchah*, which can mean consolation or comfort in terms of marriage or a home.[2] Circle the words that match that definition in the word cloud below.

True rest for our hearts is not found in any person. It's not found in a husband or a house. It's found under the wings of God, as we take our shelter in Him.

Read the following verses and circle the words or phrases that relate to rest.

> "For you have not as yet come to the rest and to the inheritance that the LORD your God is giving you." (DEUT. 12:9)

> "Blessed be the LORD who has given rest to his people Israel, according to all that he promised. Not one word has failed of all his good promise, which he spoke by Moses his servant." (1 KINGS 8:56)

> He makes me lie down in green pastures.
> He leads me beside still waters. (PSALM 23:2)

> My people will abide in a peaceful habitation,
>   in secure dwellings, and in quiet resting places. (ISA. 32:18)

On a day-to-day basis, where do you tend to seek rest for your soul?

_____

_____

_____

In Matthew 11:28–29, Jesus offers us an invitation to rest. Write out those verses below.

_____

_____

_____

The difficulties that we experience in our lives can weigh on us. Walking through life day after day, week after week with no change in sight can feel as if we're carrying a fifty-pound weight on each shoulder. Even the normal responsibilities of life can start to wear on us. *Jesus sees our tired bodies, our weary spirits, and He offers us rest.*

According to these verses in Matthew, what do we need to do in order to receive the rest that Jesus offers?

_____

_____

_____

Underline the action words the Bible associates with rest:

> Trust in the LORD with all your heart,
>   and do not lean on your own understanding. (PROV. 3:5)
>
> Do not be anxious about anything, but in everything by prayer and supplication with thanksgiving let your requests be made known to God. And the peace of God, which surpasses all understanding, will guard your hearts and your minds in Christ Jesus. (PHIL. 4:6-7)
>
> Casting all your anxieties on him, because he cares for you. (1 PET. 5:7)

So often we turn to other things to find rest. We binge-watch a TV show, relax with a book, or take a break from everyday life with a vacation. None of these things are bad in and of themselves, but they can never give us the true rest that Jesus offers.

Jesus offers us rest:

- For our _____. (Matt. 11:29)
- From _____. (Phil. 4:6-7)
- From _____. (Rom. 6:22)
- From _____. (John 16:33)

J. C. Ryle, a writer and evangelical preacher from the nineteenth century, describes the rest we get from Jesus like this:

- He will give you *rest from guilt of sin.*
- He will give you *rest from fear of law.*
- He will give you *rest from fear of hell.*
- He will give you *rest from fear of the devil.*
- He will give you *rest from fear of death.*
- He will give you *rest in the storm of affliction.*[3]

Jesus invites us to come to Him, to find rest from the troubles of this world and to restore our souls. Whatever burdens you're carrying today, Jesus knows. He knows what's weighing heavy on your heart and your mind, and He holds out His hands in invitation to give us a rest that goes far beyond a relationship or a home, as Naomi envisioned for her daughters-in-law.

How can you accept His invitation to lay down your burden and find rest in Him?

_____

_____

_____

End your study today by meditating on the words of Psalm 62:5–7, asking the Lord to help you find complete rest in Him.

> For God alone, O my soul, wait in silence,
>   for my hope is from him.
> He only is my rock and my salvation,
>   my fortress; I shall not be shaken.
> On God rests my salvation and my glory;
>   my mighty rock, my refuge is God.

Day 5: *Two Pathways*

Read Ruth 1:9–18.

When Naomi began her journey back to Bethlehem, both Ruth and Orpah were on the journey with her. Yet somewhere along the way, Naomi changed her mind and offered them a choice—to go back or to keep going. Ironically, Naomi encouraged them to return to Moab.

Reread Ruth 1:11–13. Why does Naomi encourage Ruth and Orpah to stay?

_____

_____

_____

Naomi's reason may sound strange to us. She was referring to an Old Testament law found in Deuteronomy called the levirate law, which talks about God's provision if a married man died without children (25:5–10). If that happened, the brother of the deceased had the responsibility to marry the widow. Their first son would actually carry the name of the deceased man so that his family line could be continued into the next generation. That child, raised up for the brother, would have the deceased brother's name and would inherit the deceased brother's lands.

Read the end of Ruth 1:13. What other reason does Naomi mention for wanting her daughters-in-law to stay in Moab?

_____

_____

_____

The Plight of Widows in Old Testament Times

A widow in ancient Israel was in an especially vulnerable position. With her husband gone she lost her main source of economic support. A widow was often included in the category of the poorest of the poor, along with orphans and landless immigrants (Ex. 22:21–22; Deut. 24:17, 19–21; Isa. 10:2). She often didn't have any inheritance rights. If she didn't have any children to take care of her, she was particularly vulnerable and could become a target for exploitation by others.[4]

Despite those difficult circumstances, God cares very much for widows. The Old Testament includes multiple legal codes that provided for the protection of rights for both widows and orphans (Ex. 22:22; Deut. 10:18; 24:17–22). The prophets warned against injustices toward widows and orphans (Isa. 1:17; Jer. 5:28; Mic. 2:9; Mal. 3:5), and God promised to be a Father to the fatherless and provide justice for the widow (Deut. 10:18; Psalm 68:5). In the New Testament, James says that true religious character can be measured by a person's care for the orphan and the widow (James 1:27).[5]

At first, Ruth and Orpah made the same choice; they would go with Naomi. But Orpah soon changed her mind and reversed course. Ruth, on the other hand, would not be dissuaded. She pledged her loyalty, permanently joining her future with Naomi's.

Why might these two women have made such different choices? Fill in the chart below to compare and contrast their decisions and what might have driven them.

	ORPAH	RUTH
Emotional expression		
Factors considered		
Final decision		

The choices of these two women can be seen as a picture of the way we might respond to God's invitation: stay as we are in our sin or stake all of our future—eternal and otherwise—on Him.

In 2 Corinthians 5:17, the apostle Paul describes a person who has made a genuine profession of Christ: "Therefore, if anyone is in Christ, he is a new creation. The old has passed away; behold, the new has come." How do we see this verse illustrated in Ruth's decision to go with Naomi?

_____

_____

_____

_____

_____

The choice that Ruth and Orpah faced was not only a picture of salvation but also that of surrender. On any given day we are confronted with countless choices, all of which contribute to our either surrendering to the will of God or focusing on our own comfort. We can choose to take one of two paths: 1) The path of familiarity and self-focus or 2) the path of commitment and service.

Do you think Orpah's choice reflected familiarity and self-focus? What other factors might have contributed to her decision?

_____

_____

_____

How did Ruth's choice illustrate commitment and service?

_____

_____

_____

In verse 14, the Bible says Ruth "clung" to Naomi. The Hebrew word used here is *dabaq*, the same word used in Genesis 2:24, where it says that a man should leave his mother and father and "cleave unto his wife" (KJV).[6] It means to be joined or stuck together. Ruth was staying with Naomi, and she wasn't going to let go.

Then in verses 16–17, Ruth declared her loyalty and commitment to Naomi:

> "Do not urge me to leave you or to return from following you. For where you go I will go, and where you lodge I will lodge. Your people shall be my people, and your God my God. Where you die I will die, and there will I be buried. May the LORD do so to me and more also if anything but death parts me from you."

Describe the type of commitment that Ruth is making to Naomi and to the Lord.

_____

_____

_____

What would Ruth's choice to follow Naomi likely have meant for her life?

_____

_____

_____

The pathway of commitment is seldom the way of convenience. It's often uncomfortable. Our choices, whichever way we go, influence others for generations to come. Ruth was one of the ancestors of Christ Himself. Through her faith and because she stepped out into the unknown, we are blessed today.

If you want to take the pathway of commitment and service in life, it's not something you just drift into. You have to make a choice.

Circle any words or phrases below that describe the type of choice Ruth made in following Naomi.

Deliberate	Determined	Permanent	Faith-based
Short-lived	Impulsive	Emotional	Costly

Ruth couldn't just send part of herself to Bethlehem and keep another part in Moab. Everything had to change—her environment, her friends, her relationships. Her life would never be the same.

As you read this story, ask yourself: on a daily basis are you choosing the pathway of familiarity and comfort—doing what comes naturally, easily, what your emotions tell you to do? Or are you choosing the pathway of commitment and service? Every decision we make, in little and big matters, comes down to which of these pathways we're following.

Take time to prayerfully respond to the questions below, asking God to show you which pathway you are choosing to follow on a daily basis.

Am I choosing the pathway of familiarity and comfort or the pathway of commitment and service in . . .

- My values?
- How I use my time? My money? My possessions?
- How I use my home?
- My work life?
- My relationships with family and friends?
- How I follow Jesus?

In Matthew 16:24, Jesus said, "If anyone would come after me, let him deny himself and take up his cross and follow me." If you want to be His disciple, you cannot live your life in the realm of what is familiar and comfortable.

In fact, Jesus said if you try to hold onto your life, you're going to lose it. However, if you lay it down, you're choosing the pathway of commitment and service as Jesus did for us. You may think you're giving up your rights, comfort, and convenience. You might even think you're going to be miserable. While there is a certain burden attached to taking the pathway of commitment and service, there is no joy or blessing like it. True freedom is found when we choose the path of following Jesus Christ.

Spend time meditating on and memorizing the following verse this week:

AND WE KNOW THAT
FOR THOSE WHO LOVE
— GOD —
all things
WORK TOGETHER FOR
— GOOD, —
FOR THOSE WHO ARE
CALLED ACCORDING TO
his purpose.

ROMANS 8:28

Week 3

Big Idea: WHAT WE BELIEVE ABOUT GOD IMPACTS HOW WE VIEW EVERYTHING ELSE.

INTRODUCTION

- Your boss just let you know that your position was eliminated.
- The mechanic handed you bad news in the form of a $1,200 estimate.
- The school called, and your son is in the principal's office *again*.
- Your medical test results are back, and it's not good.

How does what you believe about God affect the way you respond to these scenarios? Do you believe that He's still good, no matter what? Do you trust Him to keep His promises? Do you know for certain He has a plan for you? If we base our view of God on emotions or circumstances rather than on what the Bible says, we can become bitter and angry. We start to focus on what is missing in our lives instead of focusing on what we have. In doing so, we overlook the ways God is working in and around us.

As we continue our journey with Naomi this week, we'll see that her view of God impacted how she responded to the events of her life—and not in a good way. As we take a closer look at who the Lord truly is, we'll discover how powerful it is to have a right view of Him—of His character, His care for us, His holiness, His power, His mercy, and His grace. When you know the truth about God, it will change your life!

Day 1: *A Faulty View of God*

Read Ruth 1:19–21.

We've all experienced wounds and hurts. Often, the outcome of our lives isn't determined by *what* happens to us but by *how we respond* to what happens to us. And how we respond is determined by our view or understanding of God.

Today, we'll discover that Naomi's response to the events in her life flowed out of a faulty view of God's character.

In Ruth 1:19, what effect did Naomi's return to Bethlehem have on the town?

_____

_____

_____

Why do you think people noticed her return? Circle any reasons that could apply.

NAOMI LOOKED COMPLETELY DIFFERENT.

THE PEOPLE WERE ENCOURAGED BY NAOMI'S RETURN.

ELIMELECH AND HER TWO SONS WERE DEAD.

SHE CAME BACK WITH A MOABITE WOMAN.

NAOMI HAD BEEN EXTREMELY POPULAR WHEN SHE HAD PREVIOUSLY LIVED IN BETHLEHEM.

In verse 21, how does Naomi describe her life when she left Bethlehem for Moab?

_____

_____

_____

What was the reason Naomi's family left in the first place? (Hint: read Ruth 1:1.)

_____

_____

_____

Naomi left Bethlehem because of a food famine and she came back with a famine in her soul. She felt as if the Lord had turned against her.

When the local women asked, "Is this Naomi?" Naomi requested that they call her a different name—Mara, which means *bitter.*

What is the meaning of the name Naomi? (Hint: review Week 1, Day 2).

_____

_____

What is the meaning of the name Mara?

_____

_____

Why do you think Naomi wanted to change her name?

_____

_____

_____

What two words does Naomi use to describe God?

1.

2.

The Hebrew word for Almighty that Naomi used to refer to God is *El Shaddai*—the name that speaks of God as the all-sufficient One who pours Himself into the lives of His believing children and meets all of their needs.

The Names of God

Throughout Scripture, there are almost 1,000 names for God.[1] His names tell us what He is like. To know God's name is to know about Him and to know His heart, His ways, and His character. He will never forsake those who seek Him, wait for Him, and trust in His name.

In Ruth 1:21, Naomi refers to God as *El-Shaddai*, which means Almighty God. The first time this name of God is mentioned in the Bible is in Genesis 17:1: "When Abram was ninety-nine years old the LORD appeared to Abram and said to him, 'I am God Almighty; walk before me, and be blameless.'"

Other names of God throughout Scripture include:

- *Jehovah-Jireh:* He is our Provider (Gen. 22:13–14).
- *Jehovah-Rapha:* He is our healer (Ex. 15:26).
- *Jehovah-Nissi:* He is our banner or our victory (Ex. 17:8–15).
- *Jehovah-Shalom:* He is our peace (Judg. 6:24).
- *Jehovah-Raah:* He is our shepherd (Psalm 23:1).
- *Jehovah-Tsidkenu:* He is our righteousness (Jer. 23:6).
- *Jehovah-Shammah:* He is present (Ezek. 48:35).

Then in verse 21, she refers to God as the LORD. When LORD is written in all caps or small caps, found in the Old Testament, it stands for the Hebrew word *Yahweh*, or Jehovah. That's the personal covenant name of the God of Israel—the God who comes to meet His people in their time of need.

What did Naomi accuse the Lord of doing in her life? (vv. 20–21)

_____

_____

_____

Based on what Naomi says in these verses, what was her view of God compared to the meaning of His name?

_____

_____

_____

Naomi not only felt that she had been misnamed, but perhaps she thought God had as well. Based on these verses, it seems like she didn't think Jehovah God had met her need—that *El Shaddai* had not been all-sufficient in her life.

Have you ever felt like maybe God hasn't lived up to His name? Explain the circumstances.

_____

_____

_____

_____

Naomi made it evident that she was bitter toward God. She based those thoughts on her feelings and the tragedies she had experienced rather than the truth about God's character.

In the chart below, list what each verse says about who God is compared to what Naomi thought about Him.

	GOD'S CHARACTER	NAOMI'S VIEW
Psalm 9:10		
Psalm 48:14		
Psalm 145:9		

If someone observed your life closely, what would they say about your view of God?

_____

_____

How can having a faulty view of God affect:

• Your view of difficult circumstances?

• Your response to change?

• Your reaction when someone hurts you?

Naomi was right to believe that God was connected to her circumstances, but God wasn't her enemy—quite the opposite, in fact. As His daughter, God was *for* her. In the same way, if you are God's child, He has redeemed you. He is not your enemy; He is *for* you. He loves and cherishes you. When He brings circumstances into your life that are painful, He seeks to restore, discipline, train, and refine you so that your life can be even more fruitful.

It's one thing to *know* the names of God, to have that head knowledge, like Naomi. Yet it's another to *trust* in His names and His character and to believe that He will work the circumstances of your life for good (Rom. 8:28).

Take some time to reflect on the names and attributes of God listed below. (This is not a comprehensive list.) Choose several from the list, and write a sentence or two about how you've seen God's character revealed through your own experiences. Conclude today's study by praying through the list, asking the Lord to help you trust that He is who He says He is.

Most High God	Living God	Wonderful Counselor
King of Kings	Creator	Rock of Refuge
The Almighty	Sustainer	Helper
I Am	Father	Healer
Everlasting God	Prince of Peace	Deliverer
The Alpha and Omega	Protector/Defender	

_____

_____

_____

_____

_____

_____

Day 2: *A Bitter Heart*

Read Ruth 1:20–21.

In Charles Dickens's novel *Great Expectations*, he writes about Miss Havisham whose fiancé ran away on the day they were to be married. For decades, Miss Havisham remained in her wedding dress and veil, letting them turn to rags. She pulled heavy drapes across the windows and refused any sunlight. Instead of disposing of her wedding cake, she let it decay and get eaten by mice.

She said, "The mice have gnawed at it, and sharper teeth than teeth of mice have gnawed at me."[2]

Maybe you know what those teeth are like—the sharp edges of bitterness eating at joy and eroding away peace. Naomi could commiserate. She let the disease of bitterness eat away at her soul (Ruth 1:13, 20).

Circle words in the word cloud below that represent the characteristics of a bitter person.

Think of a character from a book or movie who radiates bitterness. How does bitterness in the character's life poison his or her relationships, emotions, or even physical appearance?

_____

_____

_____

The disease of bitterness often begins with a mild case of resentment—a feeling that we have been slighted or taken for granted. What are some wrong actions that you might take, or have taken, as the result of feeling resentment?

_____

_____

_____

_____

_____

Bitterness is often a reaction to people or circumstances that hurt us. But bitterness isn't caused by anything that happens to us. It's the fruit of our *reaction to* what happens to us— our response to hurt and to loss. And it has an enormous effect on ourselves and others.

Naomi isn't the only person in the Bible who expressed feelings of bitterness. We find another example in someone else who suffered a lot—Job.

Read Job 1:13–19; 2:7–8. What hardships did Job experience?

_____

_____

_____

Look up Job 9:17–18 and 27:2. What similarities do you find in Job and Naomi's responses to suffering?

_____

_____

_____

Both Naomi and Job experienced tremendous tragedy in their lives. In moments of sorrow, both looked for someone or something to blame. In choosing to blame God, even briefly, both allowed bitterness to creep into their hearts.

Given the same circumstances, do you think you would have responded differently than Naomi and Job? If so, how would your response have been different?

_____

_____

_____

While it can be easy to spot bitterness in others, it's often difficult to see it in ourselves. How can we know if we have bitterness in our own hearts?

_____

_____

_____

Look up the following verses and identify how we behave when we are bitter.

* _____ (JOB 7:11)

* _____ (ROM. 3:14)

* _____ (1 COR. 10:10)

Eventually, bitterness overflows. We can't keep it inside. It will come out in our words, as it did when Naomi spoke to the people in her hometown.

When we verbalize our bitterness toward God and toward our circumstances, other people become contaminated and poisoned with what's eating us. Look up Hebrews 12:15 and draw what the writer is describing.

How have you seen this play out in your own life?

_____

_____

_____

_____

_____

One helpful way to determine if we have bitterness in our heart is to ask ourselves two questions:

1. Is there anyone I haven't fully forgiven?
2. Is there any person or circumstance in my life that I've not been able to thank God for?

Take some time to contemplate the above questions and ask God to show you if there is evidence of bitterness in your own heart. If He reveals that you are harboring bitterness about someone or something, don't be discouraged—there's good news. Job didn't allow his temporary bitterness to become a permanent guest. By the end of his story, Job repented and experienced restoration. Tomorrow we're going to look at how you can get free from bitterness, too.

Day 3: *Freedom from Bitterness*

Read Ephesians 4:31.

The apostle Paul didn't mince words when it came to the subject of bitterness. In his letter to the church at Ephesus, he told the believers there to "put it away." The NIV translation says to "get rid" of it. As a Christ-follower, bitterness shouldn't have any place in our lives.

The Greek word translated "bitterness" in Ephesians 4:31 comes from the root word *pik*. It sounds like what it means—literally to prick or cut. It can refer to a sharp or pointed object or to a bitter, sharp taste. Used figuratively, it describes "that angry and resentful state of mind that can develop when we undergo troubles."[3]

Revisit Ephesians 4:31 below and circle any other emotions that go along with bitterness.

> Let all bitterness and wrath and anger and clamor and slander be put away from you, along with all malice.

Author and speaker Erin Davis describes the progression like this:

> Bitterness almost always travels in a nasty pack. When bitterness is taking root in my heart, usually wrath is, too. The same goes for anger, slander, and malice. . .
>
> - If we don't deal with bitterness, that bitterness *will* progress toward extreme anger (that's wrath).
>
> - If we don't deal with the anger, we *will* start to clamor or demand what we want.
>
> - If that doesn't work, we *will* start to talk bad about the object of our bitterness in the hopes of recruiting others to agree with and justify our feelings (that's slander).
>
> - If that goes unchecked, we *will* eventually have a desire to cause harm to the person we are bitter toward.
>
> All along the way, people are hurt, relationships are derailed, joy is stolen, and growth of the fruit of the Spirit is stunted.[4]

How have you seen this progression play out in your own life?

_____

_____

_____

_____

_____

When we allow these unwanted intruders—bitterness, anger, malice, harshness, evil speaking—to move in with us and take up residence, to be kept like harmful poisons in our kitchen cabinets, it has a significant effect on our lives, the lives of those around us, and our relationship with God.

Bitterness:
- Grieves the Spirit of God.
- Makes us hard, cold, and difficult to live with.
- Turns us into people who are negative and critical.
- Makes us resistant to God's plan and His love for us.
- Eventually destroys us, the way acid eats through the container in which it's held.

Revisit Hebrews 12:15.

What consequences of bitterness does this verse warn us about?

_____

_____

_____

Who is the intended audience for this message? (Hint: read Hebrews 3:1–6.)

_____

_____

_____

The writer of Hebrews wasn't aiming these words at those who are unbelievers and are still slaves to sin. He was writing to those who have trusted Christ and are secure in their salvation. Even if we are followers of Christ, we can still struggle with bitterness.

The apostle James gives us a clue in James 4:7–10 about how to get rid of bitterness in our lives. These methods are not simply suggestions; they're commands. They're things that as followers of Christ, we absolutely need to do.

Circle the commands that James gives in the verses below:

> Submit yourselves therefore to God. Resist the devil, and he will flee from you. Draw near to God, and he will draw near to you. Cleanse your hands, you sinners, and purify your hearts, you double-minded. Be wretched and mourn and weep. Let your laughter be turned to mourning and your joy to gloom. Humble yourselves before the Lord, and he will exalt you.

As you look upward and get to know who God is, you'll come to the place where you can trust that God has a purpose in all you've been through, and you'll trust Him to know what that purpose is even when you can't see it or understand it. As you accept His purposes for your life, you'll also realize that He has a provision of grace for your every need.

Close today's study by filling in the chart with the action steps listed in James 4:7–10 along with your thoughts about how each step helps rid your life of bitterness.

COMMAND FROM JAMES 4	EFFECT ON BITTERNESS
Example: Submit yourselves to God.	Example: Agree with God that bitterness does not belong in my heart.

Day 4: *Running on Empty?*

Read Ruth 1:21–2:1

In verse 21, what words does Naomi use to describe how she left and how she returned?

_____

_____

_____

Naomi had obviously forgotten the real state of things when she and her family had left Bethlehem ten years earlier. In what ways had Naomi's life grown even emptier during the years that she and her family were in Moab?

_____

_____

_____

List some of the things you've lost—possessions, circumstances, people—that have brought disappointment and grief.

_____

_____

_____

Read the first part of verse 22 below, then circle any words or phrases that are repeated.

> So Naomi returned, and Ruth the Moabite her daughter-in-law with her, who returned from the country of Moab.

Two times the author of Ruth tells us that Naomi returned. She was desperate—her life and heart felt empty. Perhaps she felt like her only option was to return home, empty-handed.

Now read the second part of verse 22. What was happening around the time that Naomi and Ruth arrived in Bethlehem?

_____

_____

_____

What words come to mind when you hear the word "harvest"? Circle any below.

Hope   Lack   Drought

Food   Abundance   Hard work

Celebration   Scarcity

When Naomi and her family left Bethlehem, the country was in the middle of a famine. When they returned, it was harvest season. The first chapter of Ruth contains so much sorrow, but it ends in hope. It's harvest time, a time of fruitfulness, a time for people to gather together to celebrate and be thankful.

Let's start to consider the wide range of circumstances Naomi has faced so far. At the bottom of the cup below, list the events in Naomi's life that you would describe as the most difficult.

As we end this first chapter in Ruth, we're seeing a story of how the empty becomes full. When Naomi and Elimelech left Bethlehem, they were empty because of the famine. They thought they were going to find fullness in Moab, but instead they found more heartache, sorrow, and loss.

Naomi's heart was truly empty and grieved. She had cause to be sorrowful and heavy-hearted, but she came back to her homeland with someone who loved her and was committed to her. She came home to the Promised Land, but that didn't mean God was going to make all her problems go away or that she would immediately have an easy life.

What are some ways that God was beginning to fill up the emptiness in Naomi's life? Write your answer in the top section of the cup on the previous page.

God sometimes brings us to the end of ourselves, to a place of emptiness. He chooses to make us desperate because until we get to that point, we're seldom drawn to Jesus. God wants us to cry out to Him in our emptiness and find true lasting fullness for our souls.

Are there any areas of your life that feel empty right now?

_____

_____

_____

Read Psalm 16. Draw your own cup in the space below, and then write verse 11 inside it, praying that ultimately you would be made full in Jesus.

Day 5: *Not a Coincidence*

Read Ruth 2:1–4.

So far in our study, Naomi's life has been mostly full of sadness and grief. At the beginning of chapter 2, we see a glimpse of good things to come.

What piece of information do we learn in Ruth 2:1?

_____

_____

_____

Ruth 2 introduces us to Boaz, a man who could help to redeem Naomi and Ruth's situation. Boaz is a relative of Naomi's late husband and "a man of great wealth" (NASB).

Naomi was poverty stricken and her family line was not going to continue. Her circumstances seemed hopeless. Yet generations before, God had made a way to help restore her situation.

Read Leviticus 25:25–34. What provision had God made for His people who were in situations like that of Naomi?

_____

_____

_____

Even though we've been introduced to Boaz, Naomi didn't know about him at first. What are some lessons God might have been teaching Naomi during this time?

_____

_____

_____

God had another way of providing for people in need in the Old Testament, as outlined in the verses below. As you read, underline what the provision was, then circle who it was for.

"When you reap the harvest of your land, you shall not reap your field right up to its edge, neither shall you gather the gleanings after your harvest. And you shall not strip your vineyard bare, neither shall you gather the fallen grapes of your vineyard. You shall leave them for the poor and for the sojourner: I am the LORD your God." (LEV. 19:9-10)

"When you reap your harvest in your field and forget a sheaf in the field, you shall not go back to get it. It shall be for the sojourner, the fatherless, and the widow, that the LORD your God may bless you in all the work of your hands. When you beat your olive trees, you shall not go over them again. It shall be for the sojourner, the fatherless, and the widow. When you gather the grapes of your vineyard, you shall not strip it afterward. It shall be for the sojourner, the fatherless, and the widow. You shall remember that you were a slave in the land of Egypt; therefore I command you to do this." (DEUT. 24:19-22)

How does Ruth 2:2 illustrate God's provision for Ruth and Naomi?

_____

_____

_____

Rather than expecting someone else to give them food, Ruth took the initiative. She was willing to work hard and find food to feed both herself and Naomi.

Ruth 2:3 says:

So she set out and went and gleaned in the field after the reapers, and she happened to come to the part of the field belonging to Boaz, who was of the clan of Elimelech.

How do you see God's providence (His care and guidance of all things) at work by Ruth going to this particular field?

_____

_____

_____

In those times when we feel trapped, alone, and poverty-stricken—whether literally or in our spirit—we may feel like there's no place to turn. What we don't know is what God knows: *in His way and in His time, He will provide for our needs.*

To help you reflect on times when what seemed like a series of coincidences later proved to be God providing for your needs, draw a timeline of your life below, marking those moments when God provided for your physical, emotional, or spiritual needs.

What did you learn about God's concern for you through those situations?

_____

_____

_____

_____

How does looking back over the timeline help you trust God in your current struggles?

_____

_____

_____

_____

What difference can it make as you look to the future?

_____

_____

_____

_____

What do we do when we don't see God's plan? *We have to trust.* God sometimes allows His children to experience need so that He can reveal Himself as the lover, protector, and provider of their souls. Do you identify with Ruth and Naomi in this passage—alone, needy, and confused with no place to turn for help? Do you need an understanding that God is working now?

As we end our study this week, write out a prayer below, being honest with God about any areas of life where you feel trapped, alone, or completely lost. Confess your needs and ask Him to help you trust Him to provide for those needs in His way and His time.

Spend time meditating on and memorizing the following verse this week:

the Lord REPAY YOU FOR WHAT YOU HAVE DONE, AND A full reward BE GIVEN YOU BY the Lord, the God of Israel, UNDER WHOSE wings YOU HAVE COME TO TAKE refuge!

RUTH 2:12

Week 4

A LIFE THAT SPEAKS VOLUMES

Big Idea: JESUS IS OUR REDEEMER.

INTRODUCTION

What's the worst situation you could imagine yourself in? Maybe it's losing your job, your home, and any savings you have built up. Maybe it's being separated from your family and friends—all the people who know and love you.

Now imagine if a person of influence and means saw what was going on and stepped in to help. They have the ability to get you back on track financially and reunite you with the people you love, and they are ready and willing to make it happen. Would you turn down their offer for restoration? No way!

The story of Ruth started out with heartbreaking circumstances. Last week, we saw a seed of hope—one that will blossom as we continue our study. Ruth didn't know what was going to happen, yet she faithfully served Naomi and put her trust in the Lord. Through her story, God painted a picture of true restoration.

Day 1: *A Woman of Virtue*

Read Ruth 2:5–17.

Although the name of the book we're studying is Ruth, so far we haven't spent too much time on the woman herself. Today, we're shifting our focus to Ruth and what we can learn from her example.

Based on today's passage, write a brief description of Ruth's character.

_____

_____

_____

What do you notice about Ruth compared to Naomi? Fill out the chart below to compare and contrast their lives and how they responded to their circumstances.

	NAOMI	RUTH
Circumstances		
Attitude		
View of God		

Many of the qualities we'll see in Ruth's life are the very same qualities that are listed in Proverbs 31, where we find a description of a woman of virtue, or moral excellence.

The Jewish tradition holds that King Solomon wrote Proverbs 31 as a young man after being told by his mother, Bathsheba, about his great-great grandmother Ruth. Perhaps she was describing this woman to her son, teaching him what qualities he should look for in a wife.

Look at the verses below and underline the similarity you find.

> "And now, my daughter, do not fear. I will do for you all that you request, for all the people of my town know that you *are* a virtuous woman."
> (RUTH 3:11 NKJV)
>
> Who can find a virtuous wife?
> For her worth *is* far above rubies. (PROV. 31:10 NKJV)

In both of these verses, the phrase "virtuous woman" or "virtuous wife" comes from the Hebrew phrase *chayil 'ishshah. Chayil* can also mean strong.[1]

Let's hone in on the Proverbs 31 woman's approach to work. (We will explore why this is important in more detail tomorrow.) Fill in the chart below, and then reflect on whether this is true in your own life. Jot your thoughts in the second column.

	PROVERBS 31 WOMAN	ME
Proverbs 31:13		
Proverbs 31:15		
Proverbs 31:18		
Proverbs 31:28		

Wrap up today's study by filling in the chart below, reflecting on the virtues you'd like to see God develop in your life.

LIST THE CHARACTERISTICS OF A VIRTUOUS WOMAN SHOWN IN PROVERBS 31:10-31	LIST THE QUALITIES RECORDED IN PROVERBS 31 YOU SEE IN RUTH'S LIFE.	LIST THE CHARACTER TRAITS FROM THESE PASSAGES YOU MOST WANT TO IMITATE.

Day 2: *Work as Worship*

Revisit Ruth 2:1–17.

Among Ruth's many admirable traits, one that shines through is that she was a hard worker. She was willing to go to work in the fields and glean the leftover grain—something that was considered menial and lowly work.

Make a list of the tasks and chores on your to-do list today.

-
-
-
-

When you think of the work that lies ahead, what is your general attitude? Circle all words that apply.

Privilege	Blessing	Duty
Drain	Gift	Nuisance
Obligation	Frustration	Delight

Is all work a blessing? It can be. God has given us all tasks to do, whether that be responding to emails, folding laundry, running errands, or wiping runny noses. Our attitude can make all the difference.

RECORD GENESIS 2:15 BELOW.

From whom did the assignment to work originally come?

_____

_____

_____

RECORD GENESIS 3:17, 19 BELOW.

How did work change as a result of Adam and Eve's decision to sin?

_____

_____

_____

Work is not a result of the Fall. God assigned work to Adam *before* he and Eve rebelled against God's command. Because we are sinful people, living in a fallen world, our work often feels fruitless and frustrating.

In the first chapter of Genesis, we have the example of God working as He created the world and us in His image. God didn't stop working after that. Look up the following verses and write a short description of some of the ways He's still at work today.

EPHESIANS 2:10

PHILIPPIANS 2:13

HEBREWS 13:21

As we work, we're not only accomplishing something God has given to us to do (Deut. 5:13), we're also a reflection of our working God (Gen. 1:26).

What are some other reasons why work is a blessing? Match the verses below with the corresponding reasons.

2 Thessalonians 3:10–12	Work keeps us from becoming lazy.
Ephesians 5:15–17	Work helps us provide for our families.
1 Timothy 5:8	Work gives us an opportunity to imitate Jesus.
Proverbs 21:25	Work helps us use our time wisely.
Ephesians 4:28	Work keeps us from becoming busybodies.
John 5:17	Work allows us to give to others.

When we think of working for God, we might picture something like being a missionary in a foreign country, serving in a church, or starting an orphanage. However, most of the work we do on a daily basis isn't glamorous or exciting. Like the gleaning that Ruth did, it can be menial or mindless. Proverbs 14:23 gives us a good reminder of the value of work when it's done for the Lord. Write out the verse in the space below.

List a few of the tasks that God has given you to do. How do you find profit or value in them?

MY TASKS	THEIR VALUE

In the verses below, underline instructions for how God wants us to approach work:

Whatever you do, work heartily, as for the Lord and not for men, knowing that from the Lord you will receive the inheritance as your reward. You are serving the Lord Christ. (COL. 3:23-24)

Whatever your hand finds to do, do it with your might. (ECCL. 9:10)

When we approach our work with a joyful heart, when we "work . . . as for the Lord and not for men," that work becomes an act of love for our heavenly Father—and that makes it holy work. When we're working for Him, we can see the purpose and the motivation behind our work. We do it because we love God; we do it because we love others, just like Ruth was motivated by her love for Naomi.

That doesn't necessarily make the work any easier. There will still be parts we enjoy and other parts we don't. But when we do it for our love of God and others, the load is lightened and we see our work with a different perspective. We can find our greatest joy in serving with love.

Read 1 Corinthians 15:58 below. Circle anything that encourages you.

> Therefore, my beloved brothers, be steadfast, immovable, always abounding in the work of the Lord, knowing that in the Lord your labor is not in vain.

What has God revealed about your attitude toward your own work? Are you doing it gladly or resentfully? Do you need to take more care to "do it with all your might"? What, if anything, should change in your work from this day forward? Take time to thank God for the work He's given you to do.

To close today's study, circle back to the tasks you listed in the chart above. Pray, asking God to show you how you can use each task for His glory. Write down any thoughts that come to mind in the margins around the chart.

Day 3: *Candidates for Grace*

Read Ruth 2:8-16.

One of the first steps to really walking in freedom in your relationship with Christ is to realize that this is a life you cannot live on your own. You cannot meet your own needs. You cannot protect yourself.

Make a list of the things you need help to accomplish today.

*
*
*
*

What does today's passage tell us about Boaz?

_____

_____

_____

How does Boaz greet his workers (v. 4)?

_____

_____

_____

Remember from earlier in our study that LORD (written in all caps or small caps) stands for the Hebrew word *Yahweh*, or Jehovah—the personal covenant name of the God of Israel.

What clue does this give us about how Boaz viewed God?

_____

_____

_____

Read Ruth 2:8–9 below. Underline what Boaz told Ruth to do.

> "Now, listen, my daughter, do not go to glean in another field or leave this one, but keep close to my young women. Let your eyes be on the field that they are reaping, and go after them. Have I not charged the young men not to touch you? And when you are thirsty, go to the vessels and drink what the young men have drawn."

Bible scholars often consider Boaz to be a picture of Christ and his field as one of grace. Think of grace as the place—the field—where we meet our generous Redeemer, who has gladly erased our poverty by sharing His wealth with us. Like Ruth, we are impoverished and in peril—and we are candidates for grace.

As you look at the ways that Boaz related to Ruth, compare them to the example of Jesus' relationship with us. Look up the verses in the right column, and write what they say about Jesus' relationship with us.

BOAZ'S RELATIONSHIP WITH RUTH	JESUS' RELATIONSHIP WITH US
He took the initiative. (v. 8)	John 6:44 Example: Jesus draws us to Himself.
He spoke to Ruth. (v. 8)	Hebrews 1:1–2
He promised to provide for her needs. (v. 9)	Philippians 4:19
He showed Ruth grace. (vv.10–12)	Titus 3:5
He protected her. (v. 15)	2 Thessalonians 3:3

Just as Ruth needed someone like Boaz to provide for her needs, we need Jesus to do for us what we could never do. Yet we're so prone to try to do it on our own, aren't we? We try to live this Christian life in our own effort and abilities.

Are you sometimes tempted to have your needs met by something or someone other than Jesus? To whom or what do you most often go?

_____

_____

_____

Boaz told Ruth, "Don't go and glean in another field." He was telling her not to go elsewhere to get her needs met because the Lord would provide for her right there. Although Boaz had heard of Ruth's love and devotion to Naomi and had observed her hard work, his choice to meet her needs and offer protection was all about grace.

Boaz was saying, "I know you're poor and can't meet your own needs, so stay here, and all your needs will be met." And so it is in the field of grace, at the foot of Christ's cross, where everything we need is made available to us as a gift. Nothing you do can ever earn God's favor. Ultimately, we're totally dependent on the grace of God in and through us to live the Christian life.

To close, look back at the list of what you need help with today. How does reflecting on God's grace change the way you view that list? Next to each bullet point, write "I'm a candidate for grace."

Day 4: *In the Shelter of His Wings*

Reread Ruth 2:10–13.

After Boaz generously offered to let Ruth glean in his field, Ruth responded in a way that can be both inspiring and challenging to us today.

How would you describe her response?

_____

_____

_____

Ruth was a woman with a humble heart and a grateful spirit. She didn't claim her rights. In fact, she knew that as an outsider, she didn't have any. She also had no expectations of Boaz. She went to his field simply to serve Naomi and to get food for both of them. When she received this unexpected blessing, she was incredibly thankful.

Often in our homes, workplaces, and even our churches, we have expectations of one another: "You ought to do this for me. You ought to serve me. You ought to meet my needs." What type of impact could cultivating a grateful and humble spirit like Ruth have in these areas of your life?

_____

_____

_____

_____

_____

Ruth knew that Boaz didn't owe her anything. She never forgot that she was a foreigner, that she was undeserving of favor. It's the same for us. God doesn't owe us anything. If we got what we deserved, we would be separated from God for eternity! Our salvation and any blessings we receive here on earth are completely through His grace.

Have you ever had times when you've subconsciously begun to feel like God owes you blessings?

_____

_____

_____

_____

_____

How can we guard against this type of attitude?

_____

_____

_____

As you read the following verses, what correlation do you see between Ruth's situation and our own lives before we were saved and became followers of Jesus?

> He does not deal with us according to our sins,
>   nor repay us according to our iniquities. (PSALM 103:10)
>
> He saved us, not because of works done by us in righteousness, but according to his own mercy, by the washing of regeneration and renewal of the Holy Spirit. (TITUS 3:5)

Despite the fact that Ruth had little to offer, in Ruth 2:5, Boaz took notice of her. Then in verse 11, he tells her that others in the community had noticed her as well.

What was it about Ruth that made people pay attention?

_____

_____

_____

In Ruth 2:12, Boaz says, "The LORD repay you for what you have done, and a full reward be given you by the LORD, the God of Israel, under whose wings you have come to take refuge!"

What did Boaz ask God to do for Ruth?

_____

_____

_____

Go back and read Ruth 1:9. What did Naomi want for her daughters-in-law?

_____

_____

_____

Now in Ruth 2:12, where did Boaz recognize that Ruth had found rest?

_____

_____

_____

Ruth didn't need to manipulate her circumstances. There's no sense of Ruth being frantic or in turmoil in these verses, but we do find a woman with a contented and quiet heart.

If someone observed your life as Boaz observed Ruth's, what would they conclude is the source of your security?

_____

_____

_____

Throughout the Bible, we find multiple references that speak of God's wings. Read the passages below, then match them with the description of what it means to be in the shelter of God's wings.

Psalm 17:8–9   Stillness in the midst of the storm

Psalm 36:7–8   Help and joy

Psalm 57:1   Hope in the midst of fearful circumstances

Psalm 63:7   Safety

Psalm 91:4   Refreshment

How do these verses give you hope for your current circumstances?

_____

_____

_____

_____

_____

_____

_____

How do they give you hope for the future?

_____

_____

_____

_____

_____

_____

William Cushing was a pastor and hymn writer who lived in the 1800s. After serving in ministry for many years, he suddenly lost the ability to speak. He asked God, "Hide me in the shadow of your wings" (Psalm 17:8) and wrote the hymn "Under His Wings" as a personal testimony of the security and rest a troubled soul can find only in God.[2]

As you end today, take time to reflect on the words William Cushing wrote so many years ago that are still true today. Circle "wings" each time it appears and underline phrases that indicate how knowing he was sheltered under God's wings impacted the heart of the hymn writer. Ask God for a heart that fully rests and trusts in Him.

UNDER HIS WINGS I AM SAFELY ABIDING;
    THOUGH THE NIGHT DEEPENS AND TEMPESTS ARE WILD,
STILL I CAN TRUST HIM, I KNOW HE WILL KEEP ME;
    HE HAS REDEEMED ME, AND I AM HIS CHILD.

UNDER HIS WINGS, UNDER HIS WINGS,
    WHO FROM HIS LOVE CAN SEVER?
UNDER HIS WINGS MY SOUL SHALL ABIDE,
    SAFELY ABIDE FOREVER.

UNDER HIS WINGS—WHAT A REFUGE IN SORROW!
    HOW THE HEART YEARNINGLY TURNS TO HIS REST!
OFTEN WHEN EARTH HAS NO BALM FOR MY HEALING,
    THERE I FIND COMFORT, AND THERE I AM BLEST.

UNDER HIS WINGS—OH, WHAT PRECIOUS ENJOYMENT!
    THERE WILL I HIDE TILL LIFE'S TRIALS ARE O'ER;
SHELTERED, PROTECTED, NO EVIL CAN HARM ME;
    RESTING IN JESUS I'M SAFE EVERMORE.[3]

Day 5: *Our Kinsman-Redeemer*

Read Ruth 2:18–23.

When we last saw Naomi, she was angry at the Lord and bitter about her circumstances.

Read verses 19–20. What change do you notice in Naomi's demeanor? What brought about the change?

_____

_____

_____

Record Naomi's description of herself from Ruth 1 and 2 in the chart below.

RUTH 1:13, 20-21	RUTH 2:20

What's the difference?

The word "kindness" used by Naomi in verse 20 is the Hebrew word *hesed*,[4] which means the covenant faithfulness and lovingkindness of God. As Naomi saw how God was providing for her and Ruth, both with food to eat and the field where Ruth was able to glean, Naomi realized that He had a plan for her life. In spite of the loss and sorrow she had experienced, the Lord was still showing her His love and faithfulness.

What else did Naomi realize that God was providing for her and Ruth? (Hint: see the end of verse 20.)

_____

_____

_____

Read Ruth 2:20 in multiple Bible translations. (To make this quick and easy, use an online Bible hub such as BibleGateway.com.) What different phrases are used to describe Boaz?

_____

_____

_____

In Israelite culture, if a married man died without children, the closest living male relative—called a kinsman-redeemer—had the duty to marry the widow, provide for her, bear offspring for the deceased, perpetuate the family name, and keep the inheritance and lands in the family. The Hebrew word for kinsman-redeemer is *goel*, which essentially means "protector."[5] *Goel* is the participle of the verb *ga'al*, which means to redeem.[6] In the Pentateuch, the first five books of the Bible, the *goel* was a close male relative who had the responsibility and right to act on behalf of a relative who needed help, was impoverished, in danger, or needed to be vindicated. This close male relative is also referred to as the kinsman-redeemer.[7]

Look up the following verses and write down what each one describes about the role of a kinsman-redeemer.

• Genesis 38:8

• Deuteronomy 25:5–10

• Ruth 3:9–12

In order to be a kinsman-redeemer, the person had to meet three qualifications.

1. He had to have the right to redeem—he had to be a close relative.
2. He had to have the power to redeem—he had to have the money to buy the property back or to take on this widow as his wife.
3. He had to have the willingness to redeem.

As the kinsman-redeemer of Naomi and Ruth, Boaz was a living illustration of Christ, our Redeemer. As you look up the following passages, describe how Jesus "qualified" as our Kinsman-Redeemer in each of the three aspects listed above.

1. THE RIGHT TO REDEEM (PHIL. 2:7-8)

2. THE POWER TO REDEEM (1 PET. 1:18-19)

3. THE WILLINGNESS TO REDEEM (TITUS 2:14)

End this week by expressing your thanks to Christ, our *Goel*, who is the only One who has the right, the power, and the willingness to redeem us from our sin. Go back to the list above and write Jesus a note of gratitude for His redemptive work in your life.

SIT STILL, MY DAUGHTER,

until you know how the matter will turn out.

RUTH 3:18 NKJV

Week 5

Big Idea: WE CAN TRUST JESUS TO WORK ON OUR BEHALF.

INTRODUCTION

On any given day in an elementary school classroom, you might hear some variant of the phrase, "Would you just sit still?" Children, whose young bodies abound with excess energy, find it difficult not to move around.

Even when we're all grown up, "sitting still," can be just as hard, especially when we find ourselves in trying circumstances. We want to take action, to fix things so that the outcome we're hoping for will come to pass. *Not* doing something can feel irresponsible. Yet there are times when the best thing we can do is wait to see what will happen.

This week, we'll find Ruth in such a situation. She followed Naomi's instructions, she did what she needed to do, and then Boaz asked her to do one more thing: to *wait*. She had to trust someone else to do the right thing and be patient to see how everything would turn out.

As we go through our study this week, may her example teach us to do the same thing.

Day 1: *Qualified by Need*

Read Ruth 3:1–9.

As you read today's passage, what was your first impression?

_____

_____

_____

This scene may sound kind of strange to us. Why on earth was Naomi asking Ruth to sneak up on Boaz and then lie down at his feet? Was she suggesting that Ruth seduce Boaz?

There isn't a consensus among commentators and theologians about the reasoning behind Naomi's plan. Some say this was a custom of the time[1] that's still practiced today in some Arab cultures.[2] Others notice that Naomi was strategic in the timing—close to the end of harvest when it would have been a time of celebration and after Boaz would have finished eating and drinking.[3] Regardless of Naomi's motivations, God used these circumstances as part of His redemptive plan.

Naomi lists four specific things she wanted Ruth to do in order to prepare to meet Boaz. List these instructions below:

1.   (V. 3)

2.   (V. 3)

3.   (V. 3)

4.   (V. 4)

Why do you think Naomi asked Ruth to do these things?

_____

_____

_____

As we saw through the example of the kinsman-redeemer last week, God uses the story of Ruth to point to a bigger picture that helps us to better understand both His character and our relationship with Him.

How can each of the steps that Ruth took to prepare to meet Boaz illustrate a deeper truth about our relationship with Jesus? Look up the accompanying verses to give you further insight.

1. RUTH WASHED HERSELF. (2 COR. 7:1)

2. RUTH ANOINTED HERSELF. (2 COR. 1:21-22)

3. RUTH CHANGED HER CLOTHES. (ISA. 61:10)

4. RUTH LAID DOWN AT BOAZ'S FEET AND TRUSTED HIM FOR WHAT CAME NEXT. (MATT. 16:24-27)

Write out Ruth's response to Naomi in Ruth 3:5 below.

_____

_____

_____

Read verses 6–7 below. Underline phrases that describe how closely Ruth followed Naomi's instructions.

> So she went down to the threshing floor and did just as her mother-in-law had commanded her. And when Boaz had eaten and drunk, and his heart was merry, he went to lie down at the end of the heap of grain. Then she came softly and uncovered his feet and lay down.

Now review verse 9, and answer the following questions.

> He said, "Who are you?" And she answered, "I am Ruth, your servant. Spread your wings over your servant, for you are a redeemer."

- How did Ruth describe herself?

- What did she ask Boaz to do?

- What reason did she give for her request?

Ruth might have felt that as a poor widow she was disqualified to go and approach this wealthy landowner with her request. However, it was actually her need that qualified her. In order to have a kinsman-redeemer you had to have a need—you had to be poverty stricken. If everything was going fine—you had your husband and your children and your land—you didn't need a redeemer.

We *aren't* worthy to approach the Lord to be our Redeemer. That's the point. It's our unworthiness that makes us a candidate for God's grace and for His provision as our Redeemer. We are all sinners (Rom. 3:23), and the wages (or reward) for that is death (Rom. 6:23). Yet in our unworthiness, Christ chose to take our sin upon Him and redeem us (Rom. 5:8) so that we might have eternal life (John 3:16).

What are ways that you feel unworthy to approach Jesus with your requests? List them below—and then cross out each one of them, remembering that your ability to approach Jesus has nothing to do with your worthiness. It's all because of the grace of our Kinsman-Redeemer: "For by grace you have been saved through faith. And this is not your own doing; it is the gift of God, not a result of works, so that no one may boast" (Eph. 2:8–9).

-
-
-
-

Day 2: *For You Are a Redeemer*

Review Ruth 3:9.

As part of Ruth's request to Boaz, she asked him to do something else that seems unusual to our twenty-first century minds: "Spread your wings over your servant."

Look up Ruth 3:9 in multiple translations. What words other than "wings" are used?

_____

_____

_____

Where else in the book of Ruth do we find similar language? What was the context? (Hint: Week 4, Day 4).

_____

_____

_____

Why do you think Ruth may have used these same words that Boaz spoke to her?

_____

_____

_____

This is a picture of what God does for us when He redeems us. When we come to Christ as needy sinners, we're really saying to Him, "I'm coming under Your covering. I'm letting You spread Your wings over me and take my whole messed up, sinful, broken life as Your own."

In Ezekiel 16, we read an account of God taking the nation of Israel under the protection of His wings. As you read the verses below, underline any words or phrases that are similar to ones you saw in today's passage. (The text is also double-spaced to give you plenty of room to make notes or write down questions as you read.)

"When I passed by you again and saw you, behold, you were at the age for love, and I spread the corner of my garment over you and covered your nakedness; I made my vow to you and entered into a covenant with you, declares the Lord God, and you became mine. Then I bathed you with water and washed off your blood from you and anointed you with oil. I clothed you also with embroidered cloth and shod you with fine leather. I wrapped you in fine linen and covered you with silk. And I adorned you with ornaments and put bracelets on your wrists and a chain on your neck. And I put a ring on your nose and earrings in your ears and a beautiful crown on your head. Thus you were adorned with gold and silver, and your clothing was of fine linen and silk and embroidered cloth. You ate fine flour and honey and oil. You grew exceedingly beautiful and advanced to royalty. And your renown went forth among the nations because of your beauty, for it was perfect through the splendor that I had bestowed on you, declares the Lord God." (VV. 8-14)

Go back and circle the various word pictures used throughout this passage.

Why was Israel in need of God's protection?

_____

_____

God promised to make a covenant (or agreement) with Israel. What were they instructed to do in return?

_____

_____

_____

What benefits did Israel experience as a result?

_____

_____

_____

Now let's look at the things that God did for the Israelites listed in Ezekiel 16:8–14 and compare them to the salvation we have through Jesus. As you look up the corresponding verses, describe how Jesus does something similar for us.

"I spread the corner of my garment over you and covered your nakedness."

* ISAIAH 61:10

"I made my vow to you and entered into a covenant with you."

* ROMANS 11:27

"I bathed you with water and washed off your blood from you and anointed you with oil."

* 1 JOHN 1:7, 9

"Thus you were adorned with gold and silver, and your clothing was of fine linen and silk and embroidered cloth."

• REVELATION 19:8

"You ate fine flour and honey and oil."

• PSALM 103:5

Which of the word pictures depicted in Ezekiel 16 means the most to you and why?

_____

_____

_____

_____

_____

When you come to Jesus, you come—as Ruth did to Boaz—needy and helpless to save yourself. You come to your Kinsman-Redeemer, realize your need for His mercy, and ask Him to cover you in His grace.

Meditate on Ezekiel 16:8–14, and think of it as symbolism for your redemption through Christ. Then, in your own words, use this scene to describe your personal salvation story. Tell how and where God "found you," what He did to make Himself and His love known to you, and how He changed and cleansed your life.

_____

_____

_____

_____

Day 3: A Kind Response

Read Ruth 3:10–14.

Imagine that you are Ruth, faithfully following the instructions of your mother-in-law. Make a journal entry describing how you felt as you approached the threshing floor to encounter Boaz.

_____

_____

_____

_____

_____

_____

_____

Now, put yourself in Boaz's sandals. Make a journal entry describing how you felt about your encounter with Ruth at the threshing floor.

_____

_____

_____

_____

_____

_____

_____

Thousands of years later, we have the luxury of knowing how this scene played out. However, for Ruth, obeying Naomi carried some risk.

How could this situation have ended differently?

_____

_____

_____

By obeying Naomi, who was Ruth showing that she trusted? Make a list of anyone Ruth had to trust to make this bold move:

_____

_____

_____

Let's examine Boaz's response to Ruth in verses 10–11 more closely. Using the word cloud below, circle descriptors of Boaz's response toward Ruth.

> "May you be blessed by the LORD, my daughter. You have made this last kindness greater than the first in that you have not gone after young men, whether poor or rich. And now, my daughter, do not fear. I will do for you all that you ask, for all my fellow townsmen know that you are a worthy woman."

Look up the verses below. What does each passage say about how Jesus wants us to come to Him with our requests?

MATTHEW 7:7

PHILIPPIANS 4:6-7

HEBREWS 4:16

1 JOHN 5:14-15

How is Boaz's attitude toward Ruth a picture of the heart of Jesus toward us?

_____

_____

Read Ruth 3:11. How does Boaz describe Ruth's reputation?

_____

_____

Your translation might describe Ruth as worthy, or a woman of excellence, virtuous, or a woman of noble character. This same phrase is used only two other times in the entire Bible—once in Proverbs 12:4 and then in Proverbs 31:10.

Who is someone you would describe as a "woman of noble character"? What do you admire most about her?

_____

_____

_____

Boaz was willing to be Ruth's kinsman-redeemer, but there was a situation she didn't know about. In verse 12, he told her there was a closer relative—someone who had a prior right to redeem her situation, and Boaz needed to first talk to that man.

How might Ruth have felt at this revelation?

_____

_____

Boaz goes on to give further instructions. Underline what Boaz asked Ruth to do.

> "Remain tonight, and in the morning, if he will redeem you, good; let him do it. But if he is not willing to redeem you, then, as the LORD lives, I will redeem you. Lie down until the morning."

> So she lay at his feet until the morning, but arose before one could recognize another. And he said, "Let it not be known that the woman came to the threshing floor." (VV. 13-14)

Ruth's situation hadn't changed. She was still a poor widow depending on the kindness of a man she barely knew. All she had was his word, a simple promise that he would see to it that she was redeemed. Apparently that was enough, since after Boaz's reply, Ruth laid down and went to sleep.

Had Ruth been like most of us who read these words, she would have wrestled her doubts and fears all night long. She would have calculated and recalculated how long it would take to repay his kindness. Her wonder would have dissolved into unbelief. She might even have talked herself into resenting Boaz. After all, she was his debtor—or so she might have thought.

However, we know better because we know a little about Boaz, too. He was as wealthy and generous as Ruth was poor and needy. He was a God-fearing and faithful man. He was trustworthy—his word was good.

God has promised His children far more than Boaz could have ever hoped to give Ruth. He has promised us eternal life (John 3:16), given us every blessing in heaven (Eph. 1:3), and guaranteed our inheritance (Eph. 1:13–14). That's more than enough to give our souls some rest!

What's something you need right now in your life? Have you taken the time to make your request to the Lord, pouring out your heart to Him, trusting Him to respond to you with kindness?

_____

_____

_____

_____

_____

Day 4: *Fully Satisfied*

Read Ruth 3:15–17.

As Ruth prepared to leave the threshing floor, Boaz offered her one more thing. Underline Boaz's gift.

> "Bring the garment you are wearing and hold it out." So she held it, and he measured out six measures of barley and put it on her. (v . 1 5)

Boaz continued to show grace and generosity to Ruth by providing for her needs as well as Naomi's. This gift could also be seen as a type of down payment in anticipation of all the good things that Boaz intended to share with Ruth in the future.

Record the following verses from the book of Ruth.

RUTH 1:21	RUTH 3:17

What similarities do you see? What differences?

_____

_____

_____

So often we look to people and things in our life to fill us, to satisfy us. For a moment or two, they might actually work. Ultimately, however, that feeling is fleeting. We start the cycle over again, going to food, a relationship, a job, or something else to try and fill our lives.

On the scale below, circle how often you go to Jesus first seeking to be satisfied.

NEVER   SOMETIMES   ALWAYS

1   2   3   4   5   6   7   8   9   10

What are some reasons we try to fill our lives with things other than God?

_____

_____

_____

_____

_____

Read John 10:10 below and circle the kind of life Jesus wants us to have.

| "I came that they may have life and have it abundantly."

Look up this verse in multiple translations. What words are used instead of "abundantly"?

_____

_____

_____

How would you describe what it means to have an abundant life?

_____

_____

_____

_____

_____

Now read the following verses. Underline how God's Word describes abundant life.

You make known to me the path of life;
    in your presence there is fullness of joy;
    at your right hand are pleasures forevermore. (PSALM 16:11)

As for me, I shall behold your face in righteousness;
    when I awake, I shall be satisfied with your likeness. (PSALM 17:15)

The afflicted shall eat and be satisfied;
    those who seek him shall praise the LORD!
    May your hearts live forever! (PSALM 22:26)

For from his fullness we have all received, grace upon grace. (JOHN 1:16)

From the beginning of time, people have sought to find satisfaction in things other than the Lord. At one time when Israel turned their backs on God, He issued an invitation for them to seek Him in order that they might find joy and fulfillment. In Isaiah 55:2–3, God pleaded with them:

Why do you spend your money for that which is not bread,
    and your labor for that which does not satisfy?
Listen diligently to me, and eat what is good,
    and delight yourselves in rich food.
Incline your ear, and come to me;
    hear, that your soul may live;
and I will make with you an everlasting covenant.

According to the verses above in Isaiah, what do we need to do in order to have the abundance God wants to pour into our lives?

_____

_____

_____

When Naomi came home to Bethlehem, she was returning to a place whose name literally means "house of bread," [5] yet she was hungry, empty and discontent. While she did find actual food to meet her needs, she also found the "bread of life" through a kinsman-redeemer who was a picture of Christ.

When we know Jesus as our Bread of Life, we can be filled with:

- all the _____ of _____. (EPH. 3:19)

- the _____ of _____. (PHIL. 1:11)

- the _____ of God's _____. (COL. 1:9)

Jesus Is the Great I AM

In the Old Testament, God revealed Himself to Moses through the name "I AM" (Ex. 3:14). In the Hebrew language, "I AM" is a verb, which means "to be, or to exist."[4] God was revealing Himself as the self-existent One—self-reliant and self-sufficient. He is not dependent on anything or anyone. He is unchanging and unchangeable. Nothing arises that He hasn't thought of or planned for. He's the same yesterday, today, and forever.

When Jesus came to earth, He made an astonishing claim—to be the great I AM. The Jews were outraged because they understood exactly what Jesus meant. He was claiming to be *Yahweh*, the great I AM who had revealed His name to Moses.

In the Gospel of John, Jesus says, "I AM," twenty-four times, with seven of those statements connected to a metaphor or analogy.

Jesus says:
- "I am the bread of life." (John 6:35, 41, 48, 51)
- "I am the light of the world." (John 8:12)
- "I am the door of the sheep." (John 10:7, 9)
- "I am the resurrection and the life." (John 11:25)

Jesus gives us Himself to fill up whatever we need or lack. Do you have a thirsty soul? He is living water. Do you have a hungry heart? He is the bread of life. Do you feel the weight of sin? He is the resurrection and the life. Do you feel lost? He is the way. Jesus says, "I am all that you need. I am the great I AM."

In our story of Ruth, Naomi's empty days were coming to an end, and it was *all* because of her redeemer—a man of grace who had the right, the willingness, and the power to meet her needs! We have no need to be empty either, as Jesus is ready and able to completely satisfy and fill our lives with His presence.

Are you satisfied with Christ as much as you are with other things? Ask God to search your heart and show you where you're trying to find fullness in life. Meditate on Psalm 63:1–5 below, then write it in your own words as a prayer in the space provided.

O God, you are my God; earnestly I seek you;
    my soul thirsts for you;
my flesh faints for you,
    as in a dry and weary land where there is no water.
So I have looked upon you in the sanctuary,
    beholding your power and glory.
Because your steadfast love is better than life,
    my lips will praise you.
So I will bless you as long as I live;
    in your name I will lift up my hands.
My soul will be satisfied as with fat and rich food,
    and my mouth will praise you with joyful lips.

Day 5: *Hope While You Wait*

Read Ruth 3:18.

When Ruth returned home to Naomi, what did Naomi tell her to do?

_____

_____

Briefly describe a situation in which you are waiting on someone or something right now. Is it easy for you to wait to see how things will turn out? Why or why not?

_____

_____

Although Ruth may have hoped that her nighttime venture to the threshing floor would give her a definitive answer about the future, she was being asked to wait some more.

What assurance did Naomi give to Ruth as she waited (3:18)?

_____

_____

How did Ruth know she could trust Boaz to do the right thing?

_____

_____

As we've seen elsewhere in our study, Boaz gives us a picture of Jesus, our ultimate Kinsman-Redeemer. As you look up the following verses, list how Jesus is working on our behalf today.

PHILIPPIANS 1:6

ROMANS 8:34

HEBREWS 9:24

God's request for us to wait can be one of the most difficult tasks we undertake. We want to *do something!* Yet over and over in His Word, He calls us to wait on Him, to trust Him, to sit still. God's Word says to our hearts, "You don't need to contend, manipulate, worry, or try to figure things out. Wait on the Lord and be still because your Redeemer is *not* going to rest until He has resolved the matter."

As you read these passages about waiting on God, underline the reasons why we are able to wait for God to work in our lives.

They who wait for the LORD shall renew their strength;
    they shall mount up with wings like eagles;
they shall run and not be weary;
    they shall walk and not faint. (ISA. 40:31)

Our soul waits for the LORD;
    he is our help and our shield.
For our heart is glad in him,
    because we trust in his holy name.
Let your steadfast love, O LORD, be upon us,
    even as we hope in you. (PSALM 33:20-22)

For God alone, O my soul, wait in silence,
    for my hope is from him.
He only is my rock and my salvation,
    my fortress; I shall not be shaken.
On God rests my salvation and my glory;
    my mighty rock, my refuge is God.

Trust in him at all times, O people;
    pour out your heart before him;
    God is a refuge for us. (PSALM 62:5-8)

How do these verses give you hope as you wait for God to work in your life?

_____

_____

_____

Take time to reflect on the following poem, which echoes Naomi's words to Ruth, and then write a prayer to the Lord thanking Him that He is always at work. Ask Him to teach you to wait on Him and trust that He will accomplish His will and purposes for you.

SIT STILL MY DAUGHTER, JUST SIT CALMLY STILL.

NOR DEEM THESE DAYS, THESE WAITING DAYS AS ILL.

THE ONE WHO LOVES THEE BEST, WHO PLANS THE WAY,

HATH NOT FORGOTTEN THY GREAT NEED TODAY.

AND IF HE WAITS, 'TIS SURE HE WAITS TO PROVE TO THEE,

HIS TENDER CHILDREN, HIS HEART'S DEEP LOVE.

SIT STILL MY DAUGHTER, JUST SIT CALMLY STILL.

THOU LONGEST MUCH TO KNOW THY DEAR LORD'S WILL.

WHILE ANXIOUS THOUGHTS WOULD ALMOST STEAL THEIR WAY

WITHIN BECAUSE OF HIS DELAY,

PERSUADE THYSELF IN SIMPLE FAITH TO REST

THAT HE WHO KNOWS AND LOVES WILL DO THE BEST.

JUST SIT STILL MY DAUGHTER, JUST SIT CALMLY STILL.

NOR MOVE ONE STEP, NOT EVEN ONE UNTIL HIS WAY HATH OPENED.

BY INNER BEING THEN, I'LL THEN HOW STRONG

AND WAITING DAYS NOT COUNTED THEN TOO LONG.

'TIS HARD, OH YES; 'TIS HARD, 'TIS TRUE.

BUT THEN HE GIVETH GRACE

TO COUNT THE HARDEST SPOT THE SWEETEST PLACE.[6]

Spend time meditating on and memorizing the following verse this week:

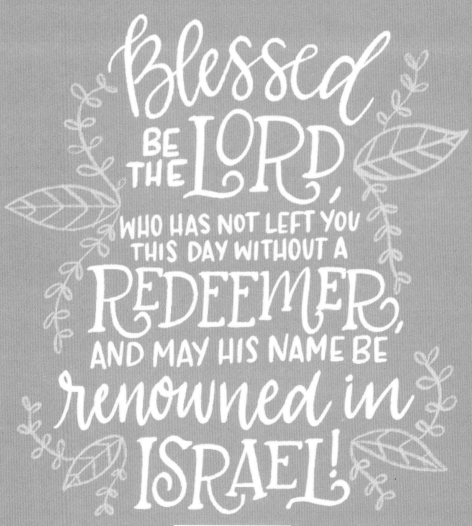

Blessed BE the LORD, WHO HAS NOT LEFT YOU THIS DAY WITHOUT A REDEEMER, AND MAY HIS NAME BE renowned in ISRAEL!

RUTH 4:14

Week 6

Big Idea: JESUS IS OUR REDEEMER AND RESTORER.

INTRODUCTION

When we turn to the last chapter of a book or watch the final movie credits roll, nothing satisfies quite like a happy ending. We want the main characters to come out on top, for justice to have prevailed, and for our heroes to ride off into the sunset.

Happy endings are God's specialty. First Corinthians 2:9 promises, "What no eye has seen, nor ear heard, nor the heart of man imagined, what God has prepared for those who love him." We've never seen anything like what God has in store for His children. Even when life is hard, we still have a bright hope and a secure eternal future. The presence of God is the destiny of every child of His.

The first part of Ruth's story seemed to have so many troubles and problems. Isn't that true of all of our stories? Born into sin. Born enemies of God. Separated from God. Yet God's grace makes a way for happy endings. It was true for Ruth. It will be true for us. We never need to lose hope that God has a happy ending in store for us.

Day 1: *Doing the Right Thing*

Read Ruth 4:1–6.

We closed the curtain on last week's study with Ruth waiting on Boaz. She didn't know what the outcome would be, but she was trusting him to do the right thing.

Write a brief synopsis of Boaz's actions in the first few verses of Ruth 4.

_____

_____

_____

_____

_____

In Ruth 3, Boaz had expressed interest in marrying Ruth. So why did he choose to seek out the closer relative?

_____

_____

_____

What's the significance of Boaz choosing to talk to the closer relative at the city gate?

_____

_____

_____

How did Boaz describe the situation? (vv. 3, 5)

_____

_____

_____

At first, the other man was willing to purchase the land. What changed his mind? (vv. 5–6)

_____

_____

_____

The situation turned out how Boaz had hoped. But it could have gone in another direction. Think of a time when choosing to do the right thing had the potential for an undesirable outcome. What did you do?

_____

_____

_____

What happened as a result?

_____

_____

_____

How has that impacted other decisions you've made since then?

_____

_____

_____

Every day we make thousands of choices. Most of these choices are small ones: What should I wear today? What are we having for dinner? Which emails do I respond to first? Whether it's a minor decision or a more major one, what we choose matters.

For each passage below, sum up in your own words what it says about how God views doing the right thing.

> Whoever walks in integrity walks securely,
>   but he who makes his ways crooked will be found out. (PROV. 10:9)

> So whoever knows the right thing to do and fails to do it, for him it is sin.
> (JAMES 4:17)

> Do not be deceived: God is not mocked, for whatever one sows, that will he also reap. For the one who sows to his own flesh will from the flesh reap corruption, but the one who sows to the Spirit will from the Spirit reap eternal life. And let us not grow weary of doing good, for in due season we will reap, if we do not give up. So then, as we have opportunity, let us do good to everyone, and especially to those who are of the household of faith. (GAL. 6:7-10)

Do you apply these principles in your everyday decision making? Why or why not?

_____

_____

_____

Daniel is an example of someone in the Bible who did the right thing in the face of difficult circumstances. As you read portions of his story, recap the events in the chart on the next page.

DANIEL'S STORY	WHAT HAPPENED
The problem (Dan. 6:6–9)	
Daniel's response (Dan. 6:10)	
The immediate result (Dan. 6:16–17)	
The ultimate outcome (Dan. 6:21–28)	

What motivated Daniel to keep praying to the Lord even in the face of possible death?

_____

_____

_____

How can Daniel's example encourage us today?

_____

_____

_____

There's another person in Scripture who gives us the ultimate example of doing the right thing—Jesus Christ. Think of the stories you know about Jesus doing what was right (i.e. obeying His Father) even when it would have been "hard" from our human perspective, then list a few of them below.

_____

_____

_____

Over and over again, we see Jesus healing people, forgiving sins, hanging out with "sinners"—while the religious leaders criticized Him, opposed Him, and ultimately caused His death. But Jesus continued to do the right thing because He came "not to do [His] own will but the will of him who sent [Him]" (John 6:38).

Write out Matthew 26:39 below.

How does this verse show the culmination of Jesus doing the right thing even when it was hard?

_____

_____

"Not my will but yours be done." In the face of excruciating pain, of taking the sins of the world upon Himself, of being separated for a time from God, Jesus chose to obey His Father. He chose to go to the cross for "the joy that was set before him" (Heb. 12:2). He made the hard decision because He knew the ultimate outcome—that we could be saved.

What do the choices of Boaz, Daniel, and Jesus have in common?

_____

_____

In our study of Ruth, Boaz didn't know the impact his choice would have—both for the immediate future and for generations to come. He only knew what the right thing to do was, and he chose to do it.

What makes it hard for you personally to do the right thing in situations that you face?

_____

_____

Ask God to help you be conscious of all of the decisions that you need to make today and for the courage and wisdom to make the right one, even if it's hard.

Day 2: *A Picture of the Gospel*

Read Ruth 4:7–10.

To complete his redemption of Naomi and Ruth's situation, Boaz took part in a custom of that time, which made the arrangement official.

List the different steps that were part of this ceremony.

Read Deuteronomy 25:5–10. In this passage what does the removal of a sandal symbolize?

_____

_____

What was the original kinsman-redeemer essentially saying by honoring this tradition?

_____

_____

As you read Ruth 4:8–10 below, mark any words or phrases that are repeated.

> So when the redeemer said to Boaz, "Buy it for yourself," he drew off his sandal. Then Boaz said to the elders and all the people, "You are witnesses this day that I have bought from the hand of Naomi all that belonged to Elimelech and all that belonged to Chilion and to Mahlon. Also Ruth the Moabite, the widow of Mahlon, I have bought to be my wife, to perpetuate the name of the dead in his inheritance, that the name of the dead may not be cut off from among his brothers and from the gate of his native place. You are witnesses this day."

Human Trafficking: An Age-Old Problem?

Human trafficking—modern slavery—is a $150 billion per year industry enslaving tens of millions of people.[1] At its core, men, women, and children are bought, sold, transported, and abused by traffickers for purposes of labor or sexual exploitation, their techniques ranging from deception to force.[2]

While we think of human trafficking as a relatively modern phenomenon, as we find in Ruth and Naomi's story, a "transaction" involving human beings as property was not uncommon in biblical times. Joseph was sold by his brothers and purchased by the household of Potiphar. Esther was a slave who was "chosen" (i.e. forced) to take part in a beauty contest that resulted in becoming a part of the king's harem.

God's Word never condones treating people as property. To the contrary, He is the defender of the weak (Psalm 68:5-6; 146:9). He is a lover of justice (Isa. 61:8). And He calls us to be as He is (Prov. 31:8-9; James 1:27).

Though victims through the ages have endured great hardship, we know God can use these immense evils for good. A brief review of Genesis 42 or the book of Esther makes clear that even in the darkest circumstances, God's plan for His people will be accomplished.

Who did the land belong to initially?

_____

_____

_____

_____

Who owned it now?

_____

_____

_____

_____

What else did Boaz say that he had "bought" or acquired?

_____

_____

_____

_____

With the removal of the other man's sandal, the agreement was complete. Ruth, Naomi, the land, and the entire family situation had been transferred to Boaz as the new owner. While it was the custom of the culture, the transfer of "ownership" of Ruth and Naomi should not be interpreted to condone the buying and selling of human beings. All people are created in God's image (Gen. 1:26–27), and any attempt to exploit other image bearers is contrary to who He has called us to be (Phil. 2:1–8).

Now read the verses below from the New Testament. Underline any words or phrases that are similar to the transaction that occurred in Ruth 4.

> Or do you not know that your body is a temple of the Holy Spirit within you, whom you have from God? You are not your own, for you were bought with a price. So glorify God in your body. (1 COR. 6:19-20)
>
> Pay careful attention to yourselves and to all the flock, in which the Holy Spirit has made you overseers, to care for the church of God, which he obtained with his own blood. (ACTS 20:28)

According to these verses to whom do we belong?

_____

_____

Who paid the price for our salvation?

_____

_____

How did Jesus "purchase" our lives?

_____

_____

What difference did Ruth's new "owner" make in her life? What would change for her from this point forward?

_____

_____

What difference does it make in our lives that we are now under the "ownership" of Jesus—both from an eternal standpoint as well as on a daily basis?

_____

_____

When you receive the gift of salvation through Jesus, your life is no longer your own. That means that your spiritual failures, your needs, and your problems are no longer your own, either. They've been taken over by your Kinsman-Redeemer. What a huge sense of relief!

It also brings a sense of responsibility. Our lives are not our own anymore. Every day is an opportunity to honor the One who paid such a high price to redeem us.

As you reflect on what Jesus did, take time to worship Him by reading the words of this age-old hymn out loud.

> I WILL SING OF MY REDEEMER
>> AND HIS WONDROUS LOVE TO ME.
>
> ON THE CRUEL CROSS HE SUFFERED
>> FROM THE CURSE TO SET ME FREE.
>
> SING, OH, SING OF MY REDEEMER,
>> WITH HIS BLOOD HE PURCHASED ME,
>
> ON THE CROSS HE SEALED MY PARDON,
>> PAID THE DEBT, AND MADE ME FREE.
>
> I WILL TELL THE WONDROUS STORY
>> HOW MY LOST ESTATE TO SAVE.
>
> IN HIS BOUNDLESS LOVE AND MERCY
>> HE THE RANSOM FREELY GAVE.
>
> I WILL PRAISE MY DEAR REDEEMER,
>> HIS TRIUMPHANT POW'R I'LL TELL,
>
> HOW THE VICTORY HE GIVETH
>> OVER SIN, AND DEATH, AND HELL.
>
> I WILL SING OF MY REDEEMER,
>> AND HIS HEAV'NLY LOVE TO ME;
>
> HE FROM DEATH TO LIFE HATH BROUGHT ME,
>> SON OF GOD WITH HIM TO BE.[3]

Day 3: *Can I Get a Witness?*

Read Ruth 4:9–12.

After Boaz finished the official business with the unnamed relative, he made a joyous announcement. How does he describe those he's talking to? (v. 9)

_____

_____

_____

Throughout both the Old and New Testaments, we find multiple references to a person being blessed. Sometimes a blessing referred to a public expression of a favored status with God. It could also express a hope or proclamation of prosperity and success.[4]

There are three common themes to blessings found in the Old Testament. First, the greater person would bless the lesser (Heb. 7:6–7). Second, a blessing was meant to be a special favor that resulted in success (Deut. 28:3–7). Third, it was a call for the Lord to bless the person (Gen. 28:3). God also promised a blessing to the righteous, for those who obeyed His commands (Deut. 28:1–14).[5] In the New Testament, a blessing was related to the close relationship that Christians experience with God as His children and members of His kingdom (Gal. 3:14; Eph. 1:3; Heb. 6:12, 15; 12:17; 1 Pet. 3:9).[6]

Write out the three blessings that the witnesses pronounced over Ruth and Boaz.

1. MAY . . .

2. MAY . . .

3. MAY . . .

The first blessing was given to Ruth. The people said, "May the LORD make the woman who is coming into your home like Rachel and Leah, who together built up the house of Israel."

Genesis 29–30 describes the life and genealogy of Rachel and Leah, two sisters both married to Jacob. Jacob's twelve children became the twelve tribes of Israel.

By invoking this blessing, what are the people praying for Ruth?

_____

_____

_____

In the second blessing, the people prayed for Boaz, "May you have standing in Ephratha and be famous in Bethlehem."

According to Genesis 35:19, by what name is the town of Ephrath also known?

_____

_____

_____

The Hebrew word for "Ephratha" means "a place of fruitfulness." Through this blessing, the people were praying for Boaz to be fruitful and prosper, both for his sake and for their town.

What is the town of Bethlehem the most famous for?

_____

_____

_____

The third blessing was for the future children that Boaz and Ruth would have together: "May your house be like the house of Perez, whom Tamar bore to Judah."

The book of the genealogy of Jesus Christ, the son of David, the son of Abraham. Abraham was the father of Isaac, and Isaac the father of Jacob, and Jacob the father of Judah and his brothers, and Judah the father of Perez and Zerah by Tamar, and Perez the father of Hezron, and Hezron the father of Ram.

The sons Perez: Hezron and Hamul. Caleb the son of Hezron fathered children by his wife Azubah, and by Jerioth; and these were her sons: Jesher, Shobab, Ardon.

Which names appear in both passages? Circle them.

The people of Bethlehem were descended from Perez, the son of Judah and Tamar. The witnesses were praying that Boaz and Ruth would establish an important family in Judah, which would result in blessing for others.

The union between Tamar and Judah was painful (Gen. 38). The whole story was a convoluted mess. But God's heart beats to the rhythm of redemption. Through this illegitimate birth, the line of Perez would extend to Boaz . . . on to David . . . and ultimately to Jesus.

That's the promise of the house of Perez. We have a redeeming God who continually makes all things new and who's always working—even through our messy lives—to write His story and display His glory.

The three blessings that the whole town pronounced over Boaz and Ruth were a corporate hope that this new family would thrive and be blessed. It was a day of joy for everyone—the givers and the receivers. And that is as it should be.

Has anyone ever pronounced a blessing over you? If so, describe the occasion.

_____

_____

To end your time today, choose someone close to you and write a blessing for them. It should contain:

* Character traits that you see and admire in them.

* Appreciation for their influence in your life.

* Your desire for them to have a joyous and peaceful life.

* Hope that they will know God and walk with him.

Then after you have written your blessing, give it to that person in writing, by saying it to them, or both. (Make sure you have a tissue handy!)

Day 4: *Disgrace to Grace*

Read Ruth 4:13–22.

What does it mean to be restored?

_____

_____

Have you ever watched a TV show where something (a home, a car, an antique) was being restored? Describe the process.

_____

_____

As you compare the end of Ruth 4:13 in light of Ruth 1:4–5, how does God bring restoration to Ruth's life?

_____

_____

What are other ways that Ruth was being restored?

_____

_____

_____

Now let's turn our attention to Naomi. In Ruth 1:13, Naomi declared that "the hand of the LORD has gone out against me." Then in Ruth 1:21, she said, "I went away full, and the LORD has brought me back empty. Why call me Naomi, when the LORD has testified against me and the Almighty has brought calamity upon me?"

Compare these statements with what the women of Bethlehem said to Naomi in Ruth 4:14–15.

_____

_____

_____

_____

_____

What has been restored to Naomi that at one time she had no hope of having or experiencing?

_____

_____

_____

How did the Lord not only restore Naomi's current situation but provide hope for her future?

_____

_____

_____

Read Ruth 4:16–17 below and mark any words or phrases that stand out to you.

> Then Naomi took the child and laid him on her lap and became his nurse. And the women of the neighborhood gave him a name, saying, "A son has been born to Naomi." They named him Obed. He was the father of Jesse, the father of David.

Why would Obed be described as the son of Naomi rather than Ruth?

_____

_____

How did Obed help to bring restoration to Naomi's life?

_____

_____

_____

In verse 18, the author of Ruth reminds us that Obed was born into the family line of Perez. As we learned from our study yesterday, out of what kind of circumstances was Perez born?

_____

_____

Now describe the circumstances surrounding the birth of Obed.

_____

_____

As you read Colossians 1:21–22 below, compare the progression of the family line of Perez to our own transformation from nonbelievers to followers of Jesus.

> And you, who once were alienated and hostile in mind, doing evil deeds, he has now reconciled in his body of flesh by his death, in order to present you holy and blameless and above reproach before him.

This family line, from Perez to Obed and eventually to David, moved from disgrace to grace. That's what Jesus does for us. He takes our start in life—enemies of God, separated from God, sinners under the curse of the Law—and He pours out His grace on us.

On a personal note, how has God changed disgrace into grace in your life?

_____

_____

_____

_____

_____

This genealogy is where the book of Ruth concludes, but it's not where the story ends. According to Matthew 1:16, who did the family line of Boaz and Ruth ultimately lead to?

_____

_____

_____

At another time in Israel's history, the people of the southern kingdom of Judah experienced a season of loss. An invasion of locusts had destroyed everything—their crops, their vineyards, their gardens. Everywhere they looked, all they could see was devastation, much like Naomi in Ruth chapter 1. The people probably felt like their situation would never change.

Yet amidst a call to return to the Lord, the prophet Joel also provided a promise—one of restoration, that God would give back all they thought had been lost.

As you read these words of hope from Joel 2:25–27, reflect on any areas of life where you have experienced loss. Ask God to bring restoration, not just by getting back any "things" you may have lost but also through an increased intimacy with Him. Then thank Him that He has the power to heal and restore our broken, frustrated lives.

"I will restore to you the years
    that the swarming locust has eaten,
the hopper, the destroyer, and the cutter,
    my great army, which I sent among you."

"You shall eat in plenty and be satisfied,
    and praise the name of the LORD your God,
    who has dealt wondrously with you.
And my people shall never again be put to shame.
You shall know that I am in the midst of Israel,
    and that I am the LORD your God and there is none else.
And my people shall never again be put to shame."

Day 5: *A Picture of Ourselves*

Read Isaiah 61.

In this last day of our study, let's take time to look in the mirror. No, we're not checking to make sure there's no spinach in our teeth or that our hair isn't sticking up in the back. Rather, let's look to find a picture of ourselves in the book of Ruth.

What are some ways you could describe Ruth's situation at the beginning of this book? Circle all descriptors that apply in the word cloud below.

What words would you use to describe how things changed once Boaz entered the scene? Circle all descriptors that apply in the word cloud below.

Now scoot up a little closer to the mirror. For each verse below, describe how it was once true of Ruth and how it was also true of us before we trusted Jesus as Savior.

> Incline your ear, O LORD, and answer me,
>   for I am poor and needy. (PSALM 86:1)

RUTH:

ME:

> But to all who did receive him, who believed in his name, he gave the right
> to become children of God, who were born, not of blood nor of the will of
> the flesh nor of the will of man, but of God. (JOHN 1:12-13)

RUTH:

ME:

> But when the fullness of time had come, God sent forth his Son, born of woman, born under the law, to redeem those who were under the law, so that we might receive adoption as sons. And because you are sons, God has sent the Spirit of his Son into our hearts, crying, "Abba! Father!" (GAL. 4:4-6)

RUTH:

ME:

> Once you were not a people, but now you are God's people; once you had not received mercy, but now you have received mercy. (1 PET. 2:10)

RUTH:

ME:

> Remember that you were at that time separated from Christ, alienated from the commonwealth of Israel and strangers to the covenants of promise, having no hope and without God in the world. (EPH. 2:12)

RUTH:

ME:

Apart from Christ, we were once like Ruth, poor and needy, hopeless and desperate. Our Kinsman-Redeemer changed everything! He offers His grace, His provision, His protection, and His love. Jesus paid the purchase price to make us His own. How does this truth lead you to respond?

_____

_____

_____

We've come a long way on our journey with Naomi and Ruth. Now that you're at the finish line, think about any themes you noticed throughout your study and list them below.

_____

_____

_____

_____

_____

As you reflect upon our study of Ruth, answer the questions below.

• What does the book of Ruth teach me about the heart, the ways, and the character of God?

• How does this story point me to Jesus and the gospel?

• In the book of Ruth, is there an example to follow or avoid? If so, how should I seek to change in response?

Flip back to the inside cover of your study book and record the biggest lesson you are taking away from the book of Ruth.

Let's end our study in the same way that we began, by meditating on the words of Isaiah 61 and praising God for healing our broken hearts, for freeing us from the bondage of sin, for providing us beauty for ashes, and for giving us joy. He has redeemed us, and He has restored us. Amen!

> I will greatly rejoice in the LORD;
>   my soul shall exult in my God,
> for he has clothed me with the garments of salvation;
>   he has covered me with the robe of righteousness,
> as a bridegroom decks himself like a priest with a beautiful headdress,
>   and as a bride adorns herself with her jewels.
> For as the earth brings forth its sprouts,
>   and as a garden causes what is sown in it to sprout up,
> so the Lord GOD will cause righteousness and praise
>   to sprout up before all the nations. (VV. 10-11)

SMALL GROUP
DISCUSSION QUESTIONS

Week 1:

- Have you ever thought that nothing good could come out of a situation, either in your own life or someone else's? Looking back, did anything good happen as a result?
- How is God specifically calling you to be a light for Him in your home and neighborhood?
- Describe how God's character is evident in troubling times right now, just as He was working in the dark days of the judges.
- How did Elimelech's choice to go to Moab rather than stay in Bethlehem affect his family? How does our choice to run away rather than stay on the path God has for us affect those around us?
- What encouragement did you find for your own difficulties in this first week of study?

Week 2:

- Who is someone you know that you might consider as "too far gone"? Pray for that person to have a personal encounter with Jesus and to be set free from sin.
- Why do we often choose to run to our "Moabs" rather than repent? Why is repenting ultimately the better choice?
- How have you found rest for your soul in Jesus throughout difficult circumstances?
- Think of a time when you chose the path of commitment and service. What did you have to turn away from to follow that path? How did God work through that decision?
- How are you personally challenged by Ruth's choice and her commitment to Naomi?

Listen in as women discuss this study in the *Women of the Bible* podcast by *Revive Our Hearts*. Find it at ReviveOurHearts.com/Ruth.

SMALL GROUP DISCUSSION QUESTIONS

Week 3:

- How has your view of God affected the way you respond to the events in your life? Did our study this week reveal any areas where you have a faulty view of Him?
- Has God given you a different perspective on the difficult circumstances of your life? What are you learning?
- Have you or someone you've known been released from bitterness? How did freedom from bitterness change things?
- Why do we often have to be desperate before we turn to God?
- How is the story of Naomi and Ruth inviting you to a deeper trust in the Lord's providence?

Week 4:

- In what ways were you challenged by the example of Ruth this week? Are there areas of life where God is calling you to make a change?
- What are some of the tasks God is currently giving you to do? How can the way that you work at those tasks be a way of worshiping the Lord?
- What consequences do you suffer when you stray from God's grace and attempt to have your needs met by someone or something else?
- In what ways have you taken refuge under the wings of the Lord? What have you experienced as a result?
- How has Jesus shown Himself to be your Kinsman-Redeemer? What does that mean to you in the present? In eternity?

Week 5:

- What do you think of Ruth's boldness in approaching Boaz at the threshing floor?
- Materially speaking, Boaz would bring nearly everything to this marriage but Ruth could bring very little. How does this represent our condition in coming to God?
- Has the story of Ruth helped you become more hopeful in any situation you are facing?
- How does Ruth's willingness to wait encourage or challenge you in your current circumstances?
- Think of a time when you tried to make things happen on your own timetable. What was the result?

Week 6:

- Can you think of a time when God restored you or someone close to you? Describe the situation.
- Through this study, what new truths have you learned?
- What familiar truths have been renewed in your mind and heart?
- What steps of action has God prompted you to take?
- Do you have a different outlook on any situation now that you didn't have when you began studying Ruth? Explain.

Notes

Week 1: Beauty from Ashes

[1] Daniel I. Block, "Who Wrote the Book of Ruth," Zondervan Academic, accessed July 7, 2020, https://zondervanacademic.com/blog/who-wrote-ruth.

[2] Chuck Swindoll, "Ruth," Insight for Living, accessed July 7, 2020, https://www.insight.org/resources/bible/the-historical-books/ruth.

[3] "Elimelech," Blue Letter Bible, accessed July 10, 2020, https://www.blueletterbible.org/lang/lexicon/lexicon.cfm?Strongs=H458&t=KJV.

[4] "Mahlon," Blue Letter Bible, accessed July 9, 2020, https://www.blueletterbible.org/lang/lexicon/lexicon.cfm?Strongs=H4248&t=KJV.

[5] "Chilion," Blue Letter Bible, accessed July 9, 2020, https://www.blueletterbible.org/lang/lexicon/lexicon.cfm?Strongs=H3630&t=KJV.

[6] "Orpah," Blue Letter Bible, accessed July 9, 2020, https://www.blueletterbible.org/lang/lexicon/lexicon.cfm?Strongs=H6204&t=KJV.

[7] "Naomi," Blue Letter Bible, accessed July 9, 2020, https://www.blueletterbible.org/lang/lexicon/lexicon.cfm?Strongs=H5281&t=KJV.

[8] "Ruth," Blue Letter Bible, accessed July 9, 2020, https://www.blueletterbible.org/lang/lexicon/lexicon.cfm?Strongs=H7327&t=KJV.

[9] "Boaz," Blue Letter Bible, accessed July 9, 2020, https://www.blueletterbible.org/lang/lexicon/lexicon.cfm?Strongs=H1162&t=KJV.

[10] "Ba'al," Blue Letter Bible, accessed July 9, 2020, https://www.blueletterbible.org/lang/lexicon/lexicon.cfm?Strongs=H1168&t=KJV.

Week 2: Coming Home

[1] "metanoia," Blue Letter Bible, accessed June 5, 2020, https://www.blueletterbible.org/lang/lexicon/lexicon.cfm?Strongs=G3340&t=KJV.

[2] "měnuwchah," Blue Letter Bible, accessed June 3, 2020, https://www.blueletterbible.org/lang/lexicon/lexicon.cfm?t=nasb&strongs=h4496.

[3] J.C. Ryle, *The True Christian*, (Evangelical Press, Darlington, UK; 1978) 74–75.

[4] Walter A. Elwell, Entry for "Widow." Evangelical Dictionary of Biblical Theology. https://www.studylight.org/dictionaries/bed/w/widow.html. 1996.

[5] Trent C. Butler, Editor, Entry for "Poor, Orphan, Widow." Holman Bible Dictionary. https://www.studylight.org/dictionaries/hbd/p/poor-orphan-widow.html. 1991.

[6] "dabaq," Blue Letter Bible, accessed June 5, 2020, https://www.blueletterbible.org/lang/lexicon/lexicon.cfm?Strongs=H1692&t=KJV.

Week 3: This Changes Everything

[1] "955 Names and Titles of God," ChristianAnswers.net, https://christiananswers.net/dictionary/namesofgod.html, Accessed June 15, 2020.

[2] Charles Dickens, *Great Expectations* (Chapman and Hall: London, 1865) 93.

[3] Lawrence O. Richards, *New International Encyclopedia of Biblical Words* (Grand Rapids: Zondervan, 1991), 127.

[4] Erin Davis, "4 Ways to Spot a Bitter Root," TrueWoman.com, https://www.reviveourhearts.com/true-woman/blog/four-ways-to-spot-a-bitter-root/.

Week 4: A Life that Speaks Volumes

1 "virtuous woman," Blue Letter Bible, accessed June 16, 2020, https://www.blueletterbible.org/search/search.cfm?Criteria=virtuous+woman&t=KJV#s=s_primary_0_1.

2 "William O. Cushing Sought to Follow Christ," Christianity.com, accessed June 18, 2020, https://www.christianity.com/church/church-history/timeline/1801-1900/william-o-cushing-sought-to-follow-christ-11630395.html.

3 William Cushing, "Under His Wings," in *Sacred Songs No. 1*, edited by Ira Sankey, James McGranahan & George C. Stebbins (New York: Biglow & Main, 1896), number 5.

4 "hesed," Blue Letter Bible, accessed June 18, 2020, https://www.blueletterbible.org/lang/lexicon/lexicon.cfm?page=5&strongs=H2617&t=ESV#lexResults.

5 Matthew George Easton, "Goel," Easton's Bible Dictionary (Thomas Nelson, 1897), accessed June 22, 2020, https://www.biblestudytools.com/dictionary/goel/.

6 Ibid.

7 "Kinsman-Redeemer," Walter A. Elwell, ed., Baker's Evangelical Dictionary of Biblical Theology. (Grand Rapids, Michigan: Baker 1996), accessed June 22, 2020, https://www.studylight.org/dictionaries/bed/k/kinsman-redeemer.html.

Week 5: All You Need

1 John MacArthur, *Joshua, Judges, & Ruth: Finally in the Land* (Nashville: Thomas Nelson; 2016) xi.

2 Chuck Swindoll, "Ruth: Interlude of Love, Part 3," Insight for Living, accessed July 5, 2020, https://insight.org/broadcasts/library.

3 Matthew Henry, *Matthew Henry's Complete Commentary of the Bible*, https://www.studylight.org/commentaries/mhm/ruth-3.html.

4 "hayah," Blue Letter Bible, accessed July 8, 2020, https://www.blueletterbible.org/lang/lexicon/lexicon.cfm?Strongs=H1961&t=KJV.

5 "Beyth Lechem", Blue Letter Bible, accessed July 10, 2020, https://www.blueletterbible.org/lang/lexicon/lexicon.cfm?Strongs=H1035&t=KJV.

6 J. Danson Smith, "Sit Still," as published in *Streams in the Desert* by L.B. Cowman (Grand Rapids, MI: Zondervan; 1997) 62–63.

Week 6: A Life Restored

[1] "Slavery Facts and Our Mission," Free the Slaves, accessed October 7, 2020, https://www.freetheslaves.net/.

[2] Definitions of Human Trafficking," childwelfare.gov (U.S. Department of Health and Human Services), accessed October 6, 2020, https://www.childwelfare.gov/pubPDFs/definitions_trafficking.pdf.

[3] Philip Paul Bliss, "I Will Sing of My Redeemer," 1876.

[4] Walter A. Elwell, ed., "Blessing," *Baker's Evangelical Dictionary of Biblical Theology* (Grand Rapids, MI: Baker Book House, 1996), accessed July 8, 2020. https://www.biblestudytools.com/dictionary/blessing/.

[5] Ibid.

[6] Trent C. Butler, ed., "Blessing and Cursing," *Holman Bible Dictionary* (Nashville: Holman, 2015), 225.

[7] "'Ephraath," Blue Letter Bible, accessed July 6, 2020, https://www.blueletterbible.org/lang/lexicon/lexicon.cfm?Strongs=H672&t=KJV.

Reflections

Reflections

Reflections

MORE FROM

Revive Our Hearts™

RADIO • EVENTS • BLOGS

LEADERS

REVIVE OUR HEARTS . COM

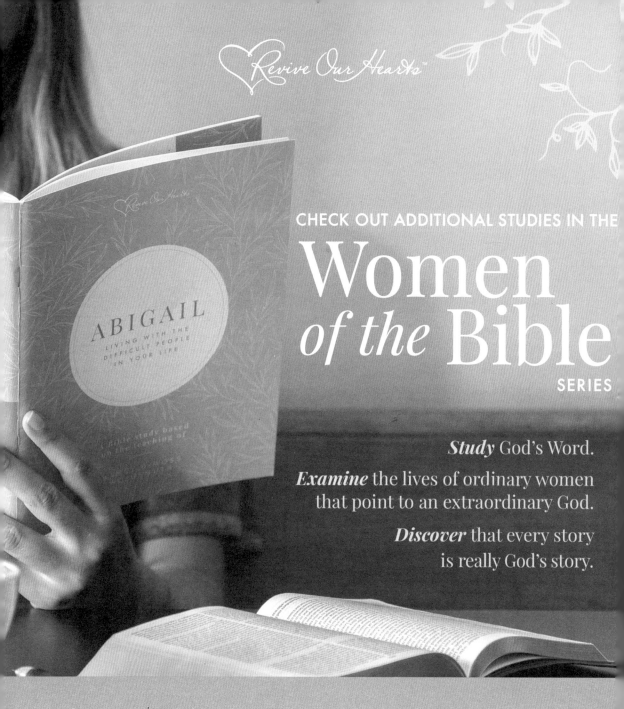